the
Colors
of Grief

Understanding a
Child's Journey
through Loss from
Birth to Adulthood

Janis A. Di Ciacco, Ph.D.

Jessica Kingsley Publishers
London and Philadelphia

First published in 2008
by Jessica Kingsley Publishers
116 Pentonville Road
London N1 9JB, UK
and
400 Market Street, Suite 400
Philadelphia, PA 19106, USA

www.jkp.com

Library of Congress Cataloging in Publication Data
Di Ciacco, Janis A.
    The colors of grief : understanding a child's journey through loss from birth to adulthood /
Janis A. Di Ciacco.
        p. cm.
    Includes bibliographical references.
    ISBN 978-1-84310-886-3 (pb : alk. paper) 1. Children and death. 2. Grief in children. I.
Title.
    BF723.D3D53 2008
    155.9'37083—dc22

                                                            2007049015

British Library Cataloguing in Publication Data
A CIP catalogue record for this book is available from the British Library

ISBN 978 1 84310 886 3

Printed and bound in the United States by
Thomson-Shore, Inc.

We do not want to lose our grief,
because our grief is bound up with our love.

Phillips Brooks, on the death of his mother, 1891

CONTENTS

PART II: Grief Through the Ages

Dedicated to all the children of the world who have suffered a significant loss. With a deep sense of gratitude, also dedicated to all who have stepped forward to join the children on their journey of a broken heart in search of healing. For as St Catherine of Siena wrote "Rouse yourself; open the eye of your understanding and look into the depth within the well of divine charity. For unless you see, you cannot love. The more you see, the more you love."

May you see loss through your heart's eyes.
May the colors of the loss weave the tapestry of the
story
Sewn with strong, loving threads of courage, hope,
and wisdom.
Whenever one door closes, may you allow another to
be opened in your heart.

PREFACE

The Colors of Grief was seeded out of a desire to reduce children's suffering in their journey through healing grief during their developmental years from infancy to the mid-twenties. This emotional journey is one of many *colors*—colors of love and sadness, courage and fear, strength and confusion; some brilliant, some dull; some dark, some bright. Colors of resilience.

Written for parents, educators, and healthcare providers, *The Colors of Grief* addresses children's shattered lives and expectations and the stages through their developmental phases, to provide practical applications to support them after a significant life loss or the death of a parent or caregiver.

In Antoine de Saint-Exupéry's *The Little Prince*, the young prince shows the grownups his masterpiece of a boa constrictor digesting an elephant and asks if they are scared. The adults respond, "Why be scared of a hat?" Grownups often fail to understand childhood grief, partially because we are misattuned to children's nonverbal communication (preverbal) about their grief experience. We superimpose our own perspective on their behavior.

Recent advances in science offer a lens into some of children's preverbal dimensions. However, as very few longitudinal studies have been done regarding children and grief, *The Colors of Grief* asks and addresses new questions surrounding these neuropsychological dimensions, in the hope of expanding ways in which we can support children.

Part I evaluates the general aspects of developmental bereavement in children, discussing:

1. the nature of a child's shattered life expectations after a significant loss, such as the death of a parent

2. the traumatic effect of losing a loved one and feeling displaced from life's normal daily routines that help to maintain physiological and psychological stability; and how physical ailment, emotional distress, and/or social dysfunction may show up later in life without attentive adult care

3. the range of emotions through the grief process

4. the stages of grief and the four phases of denial: how, unaddressed, continued denial may result in a child shrinking from change, stuck in a developmental cocoon, unable to evolve into full adult potential.

Part II maps the primary developmental stages: 0–2 years, 2–6, 6–10, and early, middle, and late adolescence. The sections include useful checklists on:

- typical developmental tasks to be mastered in each life stage in order to become healthy and successful; including physical, social, emotional, cognitive, and moral dimensions based on the child's neuropsychobiological foundation and culture

- how the child in a given developmental stage conceptualizes his or her loss

- potential problems that may arise during each developmental stage

- suggestions to support the child through each developmental stage.

Significant loss, especially the death of a parent early in development, becomes "hardwired" into a child's physical body, emotional responses, moral understanding, cognitive reasoning and perceptions, and social skills. The cumulative effects of unresolved loss can be quite damaging when not fully addressed or understood.

Drawing on the 37 years I have spent researching and working with children who have lost a parent, caregiver, or sibling, my intention is for this book to illustrate that the journey of healing a child's grief begins the day of his or her loss and ends, at the earliest, in young adulthood.

Adults often misunderstand children's unique grief experience, and superimpose their own perspective on what children's nonverbal behaviors must mean. In writing this book, I have endeavoured to write a comprehensive study of the effects of grief in children of *all* ages. It is unusual in covering not just childhood and young adulthood, but also the *preverbal* age group, *birth to two-year-olds*, from a neuro-developmental perspective. I have also utilized recent advances in neuropsychology on development of both the brain and the body (neurobiology).

The journey to healing grief weaves throughout a child's developmental years. Sometimes a child's grief is obvious and visible. Sometimes it isn't. However, it is always in the background, influencing his or her emotions, behaviors, interactions, and communication.

At its most essential core, grief for a child is a journey of the heart. The child has suffered a deep wounding. When you reach out with your heart and wrap the child in your strength, comprehending children's unique way of suffering and reacting to pain, he or she will develop a secure sense of self…and that young heart will become whole and strong at the core.

Your time and attention are a gift that will last a lifetime for that child and will result in a healthy, happy adult who is capable of deep compassion and intimacy.

ACKNOWLEDGEMENTS

This book could not have been written without the knowledge, courage, and passion of the many others who came before me, as well as those currently dedicating themselves to the research and treatment of childhood grief. Like so many books, *The Colors of Grief* is only a segment of understanding how children, at various ages, genuinely grieve the loss of those significant in their lives. They have much to teach us if we listen deeply to them and without judgment during their journey.

Words cannot express the gratitude I owe to the many people along this process of exploring developmental bereavement. To my colleague of 27 years, Dr. Gratia L. Meyer, I am indebted for her friendship and insightful understanding of the preverbal levels of development, as well as strategies designed for this source of suffering. Graduate studies and books have not discussed the preverbal years with the depth and successful intervention applications that I have had the blessing of learning while working with her.

To Dr. Ken Moses, who in 1984 offered me an enduring perspective of mourning that parents of handicapped children must live with while supporting their child and family members during the long and arduous life journey.

To the new frontier of neuroscientists, neuropsychiatrists, and neuropsychologists who join with others in various fields of endeavors to explore, share, and support one another toward understanding childhood development from the internal and external experiences of a child's world. These fields are now collaborating. Contributors such as Daniel Siegel, Allan Schore, Louis Cozolino, Daniel Goldman, C. Robert

Cloninger, B.A. van der Kolk, and Bruce Lipton have offered many of us a rich and expanding awareness of possibilities.

Writing this book in a cohesive manner could not have been achieved without the objective and insightful work of my editor, Charol Messenger, who worked with diligence and integrity. Because of her creative formatting and revisions, the readers will find the information easy to digest. It was an adventure of two heads being better than one.

Finally, *The Colors of Grief* is a tribute to my family and friends, with whom I am blessed to walk this life journey. My gratitude for their constructive opinions, suggestions, and positive encouragement, which offered me the energy and focus to persevere through this writing process. My deepest thanks to my sisters Dr. Janet J. Seahorn and Peggy E. Aschermann, and their husbands, Tony Seahorn and Jerry Aschermann, my brother John C. Di Ciacco, their families, and our now deceased parents, Charles and Ruth Di Ciacco, who taught me to see with my heart.

PART I

THE WELL OF GRIEF

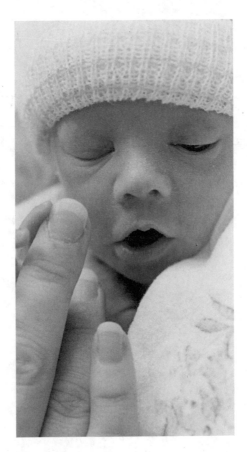

Photo by John Schoenwalter

CHAPTER 1

INTRODUCTION: SHATTERED DREAMS

Humpty Dumpty sat on a wall;
Humpty Dumpty had a great fall.
All the King's horses
And all the King's men
Couldn't put Humpty together again!

Once upon a time in a place not too far from here, and maybe not so long ago, there lived a young child adored by his parents, family, and friends. Life was moving along with a magical rhythm.

Then one morning a terrible, horrible catastrophe happened to him and, like Humpty Dumpty, he had a very *big* fall. Someone never returned, a very important, very precious person to who he was and who he would become—a critical, essential person in his everyday life. A dark, looming cloud fell over his world, forcing him to take a journey of recovery from his very deep wound.

Expectations of future experiences are embedded with significant others—whether a parent, sibling, pet, friend, or familiar surrounding. Dr. Ken Moses, a leading grief psychologist, has said that any life loss shatters one's dreams.

The irrevocable loss of a parent or any beloved is heartbreaking at any age but for a child, losing a primary caregiver—especially the mother, especially when young—can be the most difficult grief to heal, because the child's entire life picture has drastically shifted. His[1] world has shattered. His beliefs have been shaken. Expectations have been destroyed. Flooded with strong or confusing emotions, the child may shut down, or even fall into despair. Raw emotions abound. Infants cry. Toddlers throw tantrums.

Stripped bare, life is now filled with uncertainty. Lost is the life rudder by which to negotiate the world. *The Colors of Grief* offers new tools to help you (whether caregiver, educator, or clinician) help children do just that.

Psychologists and scientists address the trials and tribulations of a child's loss by using developmental aspects in the following domains: neurological (nervous system and brain functioning), psychological (how the child feels and thinks; emotions, responses, attitudes), cognitive (ability to think, reason, and remember), and moral (societal, cultural, and personal rules and norms utilized to preserve life). The various scientific terms relating to a child's development that you will find in this book may sound complicated (see Glossary for useful definitions), but they simply relate to the fact that the little one is developing and expanding trust in himself, others, and the world—with the help of a loving, nurturing environment provided by significant caregivers (e.g. family, adoptive parents, counselors).

Children are not like adults, and only adults can help them learn to live again in fullness and in joy…to trust again. So, they need to be taught and guided with an astute and learned perception of their unique process through grief and pain.

Grief is a long and difficult journey during the years a child is growing up. The goal of this journey—to heal the deep grief—is to keep the last three lines of the Humpty Dumpty rhyme from ever occurring!

The loss of a parent or significant other is felt at a deep, visceral level—in body, mind, and spirit. No words can soothe. Only a deep listening presence soothes a child's suffering.

A child's shattered life and shattered dreams can be put back together, but it takes a very magical glue, hidden from sight, in a child's wordless, preverbal world of body and brain. Your "caregiver glue"

---

1   The use of personal pronouns will alternate between *he* and *she*, etc. across chapters throughout this book and within the appendices.

adheres gently and snugly to support the child through his expanding years, and he deeply and keenly feels this glue that closely connects you both:

Be emotionally present, and physically present. Be available throughout the long journey.

Be resilient, with steadfast care, attentiveness, and heartfelt wisdom.

Mind you, this glue takes a long time to set, but once set, by young adulthood the child has developed a strong, secure core self.

Like all good stories, this one *can* have a happy ending.

CHAPTER 2

LOSS AND SEPARATION

We must accept finite disappointment, but we must never lose infinite hope.—Martin Luther King

Grief is not logical. No one chooses to be sad. One just feels it. Grief engulfs us like a sudden eruption as our heart spills over. At any age, grief feels like "the dark night of the soul," the downside of life (Parkes 1983).

A child's early years are critical for a healthy development (cognitive, social/emotional, moral), to form a strong foundation that will serve as a barometer by which to measure life's events and to make safe and reasonable choices. Without this healthy psychological foundation—if there is any intrusion into a child's belief that life is safe—a child will be vulnerable to developing misconceptions about how to behave, interact, avoid harm, and will find it difficult to become who she actually is. A significant loss can incur a deep psychological wound that sharply alters the child's worldview and requires intervention to adjust that child's expectations about life, to give her coping skills for future disappointments and to avoid missteps.

With a trauma, a child unconsciously builds an invisible wall to hide her pain and shut out terror. This shields the child until she can develop a more mature level and learn to face her agony from the loss. By the mid-twenties, a person is generally able to understand death and loss, because the brain has developed and is now able to evaluate life in a more sophisticated manner using abstract reasoning. Someone who has experienced trauma as a child is able to view the past loss from a wider lens and with increased perspectives from various viewpoints, and coping skills support the management of emotions with a core sense of safety. All of these reduce the risk and the feeling of fragmentation and the fear of abandonment.

When uprooted, children live as if in shadow; they become chained to their fears. Healing comes as a child learns to manage sorrow and uncertainty and gains perspective.

There is no easy way to do this. So, anything you can do to alleviate a child's distress is a responsibility. Grieving children need encouragement. "Like plants need water and sunshine, children need a supportive adult to hold their tears and fears" (Dreikur and Stolz 1987).

When a child's psychological development is interrupted by the death of the mother or significant caretaker (whether father, grandparent, nanny, foster parent, or carer), or if the home is destroyed whether through abandonment, adoption, divorce, or a disaster, the grief process begins a long journey of repairing the mind, body, and spirit.

With death and danger pervasive in society, few people get through childhood or adolescence without some kind of fear affecting their worldview, self-esteem, self-confidence, and expectations, so how to re-establish their feeling of trust is crucial.

Learning to negotiate grief is like trying to climb out of a deep well. Children cannot do it alone. They feel dark shadows around them. Provide guidance and support to help them relearn who they are, that they *are* safe again, that they *are* loved and can love again.

BONDING AND ATTACHING

Premature twins born in New York City several years ago were separated at birth; the boy was weaker, his sister, stronger. Placed in a separate incubator—in a separate part of the intensive care unit—the boy began to deteriorate. Breaking protocol, the nurse put him into the same incubator as his twin sister. Instantly, the premature girl put her right hand over to him and held him. Immediately, the boy began to stabilize.

Over the years, parents of twins have reported similar stories at my seminars, about when one of their infants was in the hospital and deteriorating. Amazing recoveries began as soon as the twins were reunited. The twins were joined through a web of hidden regulators.

We connect with the first person we are near, usually our mother—our first emotional attachment, the glue that holds mother and infant together. In the story *The Little Prince*, a model of attaching in relationship, the fox says to the little boy, "Now here is my...very simple secret. It is only with the heart that one can see rightly."

As an infant, the closer our attachment to a person (or pet), the more our hidden regulators are woven through our daily routines, daily influences, and sensory connections to the world—which provide a sense of continuity. These regulators create an anticipation and expectation that the daily activities will be regular, consistent, and predictable.

To lose the primary caretaker as an infant shocks the undeveloped mind and body and instills a lingering fear of abandonment. Death of the mother or significant caregiver can leave a hole for life, if not replaced with love and familiar regulators.

The most critical phase of setting lifelong patterns occurs during the first year of life. From birth to nine months, we are in the process of creating mental representations of our caregivers. At the preverbal age (0–3 years), we are unable to express through words and explicit memories the overwhelming impact of a loss on our life. Forever after, we try to solve the puzzle "What specifically was lost?" in order to fill the void inside.

Any loss during the early months of life affects the core personality. Losing the primary caretaker—especially the mother—and the inevitable changes in the daily routines creates uncertainty. With the safety net gone and the life rhythm disrupted, the child's world is shattered.

Even with a healthy attachment to others, losing a beloved breaks the heart and the dream of togetherness comes to a halt.

THE UNIQUENESS
OF CHILDHOOD BEREAVEMENT

Loss and grief are universal. No one escapes loss in life. Through suffering, we deeply join with each other. It is a common human experience.

However, through this journey we learn how to evolve and dissolve false beliefs, thoughts, and memories, let go of harmful emotions, and recognize our body's signals through pain and sensations, toward becoming healthy emotionally and physically.

Childhood bereavement is quite different from adult bereavement. It is like comparing apples with oranges. Adults have lived multiple experiences and developed coping mechanisms to handle their losses. The adult brain is fully developed and capable of reasoning abstractly. However, children are still in the process of developing: physically, cognitively, emotionally, and morally. They lack the experience and brain development to handle a significant loss.

Coping with childhood bereavement involves an interplay between a child's developmental tasks as they grow, and conflicts at each phase and transition. Their lack of experience with loss and undeveloped coping skills cause them to be more vulnerable in ways adults are not. Heightened separation anxiety and feelings of insecurity, mistrust, abandonment, alienation, and annihilation can be the result of a vulnerability created by an early loss in life. A past loss can shadow and complicate a new loss, creating more stress.

Brain development allows each of us to mature in our thought, behavior, regulation of emotions, and social skills. Because children's brains are still developing, their awareness about loss and death progresses through the years, so their coping skills are more restricted the younger they are and it takes time for them to learn while their brains develop.

Bereavement superimposed over a child's usual developmental tasks are an additional life challenge for them. A loss in childhood is a double whammy—with the risk of falling behind in their emerging developmental normal life demands, and a risk of getting stuck in their grief.

Stroebe and Schut (1999) described the effect of this well:

> Children shift back and forth between grief and engagement—a dual process of "loss orientation" dealing with and processing various aspects of the loss experience, and "restoration orientation" of adapting to the demanding changes triggered by the loss while trying to cope with the many activities of daily life. (p.216)

For an individual to become successful in her particular society, various developmental tasks—major life phases defined by the culture—need to be mastered at specific stages. In the field of pediatric neuroscience (child's brain development), we do not yet know which tasks are specifically critical windows of opportunity or sensitive periods.

A critical period is a window of time during which a specific part of a child's developing brain is open to stimulation, after which it closes forever. Critical periods are a very specific "use it or lose it" opportunity in early life (Schore 2003a, 2003b). Neurobiological (brain-body) researchers have confirmed functions that develop during these critical periods, including vision and speech. Recently, an emotional critical period was identified in the area of regulating emotions (affect regulation).

"Sensitive period" is a phrase used primarily by psychologists to describe a less precise period of time when certain functions are most readily developed, but which may not be lost forever if not developed at that time. Examples of these functions include learning a second language or math, and developing logic.

Adults who care for children who have incurred a significant loss must therefore first identify the child's stage of development and the developmental tasks in that stage, then provide to the child support and intervention so the development remains on schedule toward becoming a healthy and stable adult. A child's failure to master these tasks at any particular developmental stage can lead to greater difficulty later in life, particularly in coping with new loss (Havighurst and DeHann 1957). Learn to comprehend the child's relationship with the person, pet, or significant circumstance now gone; and address her loss at the developmental level appropriate to her.

EFFECTS ON THE CHILD'S HEALTH OVER THE YEARS

Early separation induces a susceptibility to physical disturbances. "The body bears the burden," wrote Dr. Robert Scaer (2005); "The body keeps the score," wrote van der Kolk, McFarline, and Weisaeth (2006).

Infants develop preferences for highly specific sensory features in a significant other, known as "hidden regulators" because they affect the pattern of the infant's physiological activity and development. The early withdrawal of the mother's hidden regulators (even at 15 days of age) alters the natural course of a child's physical development. Chronic stress increases toxicity in developing organs; which may result in gastro-intestinal diseases later in life, or a predisposition to gastric ulcers or tumors; or a cardiovascular, endocrine, or immune disorder. Infants separated from their mothers show acute behavioral and physiological changes; including high-frequency vocalization, hyperactivity, decreased growth hormone, and increased corticosterone levels (Hofer 1996). Considerable evidence suggests that severe early stressors can affect one's physiological development and susceptibility to disease.

Longer separations result in social withdrawal, depression, and appetite changes. Long-term physiological changes may even directly result from the deprivation of the mother's influence (Anisman *et al.* 1998; Gunnar 2005; Hofer 1996; Kopp and Rethelyi 2004; Luecken 2000; Luecken *et al.* 2006; Maunder and Hunter 2001; O'Conner 2005; Perry 1993; Pesonen *et al.* 2007). Separation of the mother simultaneously with withdrawal of the mother's regulating interactions may result in a maladaptive (see Glossary) development and increased predisposition to disease, because the infant's physiological and behavioral systems depend on them for healthy, adaptive development.

Research studies in this field have consistently shown that parental loss in childhood and the absence of a warm, quality caretaker does effect depression as an adult (Cozolino 2002; De Bellis *et al.* 1999a, 1999b; Meany 2001). To grow up psychologically healthy, a young child needs a warm, intimate, consistent, and predictable relationship with her own mother or at least a "permanent mother substitute" (Bowlby 1951). Psychologists refer to this parent–infant relationship as "secure attachment"—an emotional bond that is powerful and long-lasting. The absence of a good attachment figure may result in short-term hormonal problems and long-term neurobiological (mind-body) alterations that may predispose the individual to psychopathology (emotional disturbance). Research suggests that an early disruption in an attachment relationship is also related to altered cardiovascular and neurohormonal problems in adults (Luecken 1998).

Early attachment loss can also result in insecurity as an adult, increased susceptibility to stress, and help-seeking behavior. A growing body of evidence describes a high prevalence of psychological traumas in the past in those with a variety of health problems now, including gastrointestinal disorder, fibromyalgia, and chronic pain. Clinical observations have revealed that trauma, neglect, parental loss, and separation increase in the risk of insecurity as an adult (Maunder and Hunter 2001).

While brief separation as an infant from the mother may result in protest behavior (such as screaming, agitated searching, excessive self-grooming), persistent separation may result in curbed responsiveness, lower heart rate, lowered body temperature, and/or despair (Bowlby 1981). Without a consistent and predictable caregiver, isolation-rearing can result in disorganized social behavior, which may create abnormalities in neurotransmitters and hormonal functions, and a reduction in cerebral (brain) and motor skills.

SOCIAL DYSFUNCTION
AND ATTACHMENT DISORDERS

In a study involving 123 human babies, Rene Spitz (1945a, 1945b) explored the lack of development in institutionalized children who, for various reasons, had been removed from their mothers early in life. Some had been placed with foster families; others were raised in institutions, such as orphanages, foundling homes, or nursing homes without a family atmosphere.

The nursing-home babies were attended by nurses on eight-hour shifts. A third of these babies died; 21 were still living in an institution after 40 years. Most were physically, mentally, and/or socially retarded.

The importance of the social environment was demonstrated in a study by Harry and Margaret Harlow (1966). In a laboratory setting, they discovered that a baby monkey raised on a bare wire-mesh cage floor survives with difficulty, if at all, during the first five days of life. The Harlows then created various surrogate mothers, ranging from wire only (minimal capability for contact comfort) to one with terry cloth; then adding a light bulb to radiate heat (i.e. increasing a surrogate with maximal capability for contact comfort). The resulting data indicate that contact comfort with the mother figure was absolutely important in the development of affectional responses, to the point that the baby much preferred the nonlactating cloth mother over the lactating wire mother.

In this social-isolation study, the monkeys developed bizarre behavior, accompanied by a significant lack of affectional response. They frantically and continuously clutched at their bodies with a common anxious behavior, both in and out of a crouched position. Inconsolable, they screamed and cried, bit and tore at themselves and other objects, intensely rocked and banged their heads.

Studies such as this have documented that human children, like most animals that have skin, need both physical and emotional contact throughout their lives—and it is critical during developing years. Physical contact is vital to infant growth and development. It is a rich hidden regulator that offers the child information about hot and cold temperatures, security and pain, motion, and positioning in the available space. Without touch, a significant loss intensifies the response of separation and feelings of fear and anxiety, which can result in hallucinations, extreme apathy or anxiety, losing the sense of self, and disorder in relationship attachments.

One essential function of a caregiver is to provide a haven of safety for an infant in a time of fear and/or danger. A healthy personality results from a living model that mentors the child's behavior whenever she perceives a threat. A child's beliefs are based on expectations of self and others.

Depending on the degree of isolation and nature of interactions, infants that lack a quality caregiver after a significant loss are at risk of developing an "insecure attachment disorder." There are three subtypes:

- *Avoidant attachment personality* ("I'm okay. You're not."). Often distrusts others, but has a positive view of self and emphasizes independence and self-sufficiency. Highly values an undemanding attitude. Avoids intimacy with others, while suffering underlying insecurity. Situations that demand relinquishing control, dependence on others (e.g. illness), and demands for intimacy often result in crisis. Avoidant children are competitive, seem cold to others, and are dismissive about their own and others' emotions.

- *Preoccupied anxious/ambivalent attachment personality* ("You're okay. I'm not."). Associated with excessive care-seeking, separation protest, fear of loss, and rage reactions at any trigger of potential abandonment. Seeks care, but the soothing result from contact is partial and transient. Preoccupied children are anxious, overly dependent, emotional, impulsive, and seek approval.

- *Disorganized/chaotic attachment personality* ("I'm not okay. You're not okay."). A state of perpetual fearfulness, caution, doubt, self-consciousness, shyness, suspicion; in times of extreme stress, psychosis. Chaotic children are at high risk for dissociation, because their primary defense mechanism and sense of self is easily fragmented under stress.

HIDDEN REGULATORS WRAPPED IN EVERYDAY LIFE'S ROUTINES

In the early days, months, and years of life, so much about how children perceive the world is shaped by their daily routines, what happens in their environment, and how they are treated, and by their senses (what they see, hear, smell, taste, touch).

A child's rhythm of life is based on her hidden regulators, which over time create mental images of the caregivers (Hofer 1984). For example, in my work, I have encountered many children adopted from China who traveled many miles to connect with their adoptive parents. These children are often found to be wearing three to four layers of clothing even in the heat of August. When the new parents take the child up to the hotel room, some parents began to remove often smelly, sweaty, and dirty layers of clothes and bathe the naked child, believing that doing so will allow their newly adopted daughter or son to feel much better. But with each layer of clothes being removed, the child experiences a "derobement" of familiarity, the hidden regulators wrapped in these pieces of clothing—familiar scents; textures that were stroked, twisted, and pulled; temperatures and weight from the layers; colors and patterns which were visually explored; and tastes from sucking and picking. The hidden regulators of familiarity serve a role similar to Linus' security blanket in the Peanuts comic strip. Stripped of her clothing, the child's physical loss generates a deep insecurity. So much of what she knew is gone, and so much of what is present is foreign. Most of these infants and toddlers have never seen a bathtub. With the child dressed in fresh, lighter garments, the adoptive parents believe the child now feels better and more comfortable. However, the unfamiliar sensory experiences of bathing and drying by different caregivers is totally new. Gone are the hidden regulators by which the child has held onto the familiar past memories. The layers of clothing contained connections to home and family, safety and security. It is all gone, tossed away as insignificant, a mass of germs, as in the story of the

"Velveteen Rabbit" who was thrown out by the nanny to be burned when the little boy who made the rabbit *real* recovered from a serious illness. Throughout the boy's illness, the bunny had snuggled closely, knowing "the Boy needed him."

Throughout young children's lives, their clothing snuggles them in familiarity. New surroundings are unfamiliar (new place, new caregiver, new ways of doing things). The rhythm of life has changed. Gone are the siblings, playmates, and adults who were part of the child's world.

We, too, know the sensations when our own hidden regulators are missing. It is called "sensory deprivation." Ever been up for several nights in a row studying or caring for someone? Ever experience a change in work shift from night to day? Ever travel across time zones and experience jet lag? Sensory deprivation (i.e. hidden regulators that became dysregulated) can manifest as decreased vigilance, decreased attention span, sleep disturbance, fatigue, weakness, agitation, or depression. The similarities between these symptoms and the chronic background symptoms of bereavement are striking.

Many young children in this situation go into shock and numbness. There is too much to take in all at once, and they withdraw. Some scream, kick, bite, or cry incessantly at the loss of familiar surroundings. They have the energy to fight in the hope of returning to their lost surroundings. Such behaviors are manifestations of Bowlby's (1973) stage described as "protest and despair."

One recent August, in a plane on my way to a speaking event, I watched a beautiful, 14-month-old, newly adopted Chinese girl dressed in a pink-and-white sundress. The new mother began tickling the girl's bare feet. I watched in amazement as the child never twitched a muscle and remained lethargic and unresponsive. The father then lifted her up onto his shoulder to see around the plane. She gazed through the rows back and forth, searching for a familiar Asian face. When she found none, she slumped back into his arms and went to sleep. At the airport, many people welcomed the child with balloons and stuffed animals. However, she retreated with a glazed look, overwhelmed by too much newness and too few familiar landmarks by which to feel comfortable in meeting these new people in her life.

Increased activity during transitions like this one—as well as a new home, new daycare, new school—often make children anxious.

Sometimes, clinicians are brought in as a daycare worker or teacher, who believe that the child has an attention deficit hyperactivity disorder (ADHD). Although the behaviors are similar, displaced children can actually be suffering from "separation anxiety." So, it is essential that clinicians visit such children in a variety of settings and take thorough histories to understand each child's traumas. When I revisit daycare centers and schools two or three months after a supportive intervention, the children are often focused and are helping the other children who are restless, hyper, and inattentive.

Familiar routines are the stuff of life, from the first day we see our mother's face. As an infant, we do not judge our caregivers; we experience them, good, bad, or ugly in our interactions. A frown instead of a smile by the parent can shape a feeling of fear and anxiety. Not being held with love during the early years can create a craving for love, or a withdrawing from love, which builds an expectation throughout one's entire life.

Much of what we do, feel, and think is based on our earliest interactions and routines: morning and bedtime rituals, how we are fed and bathed, whether we are acknowledged or dismissed, how we are spoken to, soothed, and played with. The mother's behavior and interaction determine an infant *feeling felt* (Siegel 1999, p.89), called "attunement" (see Glossary) in psychology, the experience of being understood by another. The caregiver can read the unspoken cues of the child, thereby increasing the possibility of satisfying the needs based on the child's developmental level. *Feeling felt* interactions during the first two years of life build a foundation for secure attachment and empathy. Interactions such as feeding and diapering, repeated over time, (e.g. mother's smell, sound, look) become linked in memory, so specific cues denote mother. All of these shape a child's outlook on life...their behavior and emotional patterns, the regulators through which they discern and anticipate all future experiences.

The premature loss of one's mother (her presence and interactions) can produce a major shift physiologically, making the child susceptible to deep (pathological) sadness; evidenced in disturbed sleep, poor appetite, or health disorders (e.g. weakened cardiovascular, endocrine, or immune system; painful menstrual periods). With a bereaved child, the deprivation of familiar sensory stimuli and the lost daily rhythm may cause a biological imbalance, because the regulators had become hardwired into the body's neurophysiological system.

Losing the routines leaves a child without any anchor by which to feel steady, without a compass by which to feel a sense of direction. Whenever the daily routines are altered through an unexpected event, especially the death of the mother or father, this shocking loss of the familiar in the child's young world destroys her sense of normalcy. Life as it was has ended, and the child feels completely at life's mercy.

The terrifying fear must be immediately attended, so that it does not root deep into beliefs and feelings that will reshape the child's entire life. Re-establishing familiar routines (e.g. time and place) restores the sense of security and physical stability. To calm a separated infant or child, reintroduce the familiar hidden regulators (sights, sounds, smells, tastes, textures, touches) with which the child associates comfort.

The sooner the life patterns and rhythms are restored, the sooner the bereaved child resumes a feeling of normalcy. This is crucial for the very young, because they have not yet established a sense of personal identity.

CHAPTER 3

THE PRISM OF EMOTIONS THROUGH THE GRIEF PROCESS

Developmental grief through childhood is like a beam of white light through a prism. The journey comprises a full spectrum of emotions that manifest in behaviors. Each color in the spectrum of light is only a component of the white light, even though it may be seen separately. Similarly, each physical sensation, thought, emotion, and behavior is a component of the entire child in that moment.

One cannot eliminate colors from a prism. Likewise, we cannot eliminate or avoid specific physical feelings, thoughts, emotions, or behaviors experienced during grief. Just as white light comprises all colors, so a child's good, bad, and ugly emotions, outbursts, and behaviors comprise his full experience and expression of himself. The use of courage and strength to acknowledge the difficult emotions of grief through the child's ages toward maturity can lead to an adult who is healthy, stable, and happy—with the help of patient and attentive caregivers.

FEAR AND ANXIETY

A child may fear the dark or the boogeyman. Anxiety is a symptom of fear and, thus, grief. Fear is an unpleasant feeling of a perceived risk or danger, real or not. It is a basic, primary emotion. Fear is the feeling of vulnerability, annihilation, abandonment. Anxiety is a feeling of apprehension, uncertainty, and fear without apparent stimulus. Fear and anxiety are associated with physiological changes (e.g. sweating, tremor, rapid heart rate).

With *healthy* fear, we stop and pay attention to the *present* moment. We recognize that something isn't quite right. This innate response is a mechanism for survival that begins at birth. A warning triggers inside (e.g. jumping at the sight of a snake). We immediately go into action to respond to the unexpected situation.

When a young child feels vulnerable, he cannot differentiate reality from fantasy, and the fears exhibited may seem illogical to the adults. Nevertheless, it is important to acknowledge a child's fears empathetically as legitimate *and* to support the child's behavior, not dismiss it.

A new trauma that resembles a past experience often triggers fear and anxiety. The caregiver may not know the underlying cause. However, observing the child's behavior can offer glimpses and help you determine an approach or treatment. Remember, all significant, powerful experiences are imprinted in the implicit or unconscious memory, even from as early as *in utero*.

Anxiety becomes a block when a child feels overloaded and cannot think his way through the dilemma. He may behave aggressively toward self or others, or may totally withdraw. If left to his own immature capacities, the stress can move the child to a severe level, causing him to become immobilized and to dissociate from the overwhelming and agonizing experience.

It isn't hard to overstress a young, immature brain and body. Very young children need a mature adult to support them in negotiating the new world. When insecure, they can feel that everything is life-threatening. If a trauma is triggered over and over, without someone to help to lower the threat and create a haven of safety, the child can disintegrate into extreme sensitivity, hyperarousal, hyperactivity, a tendency to misperceive threats, or to act out. Neuroscientist Joseph LeDoux (1996) explained it this way:

> Unconscious fear memories established through the amygdala appear to be indelibly burned into the brain. They are probably with us for life. This is often very useful, especially in a stable, unchanging world, since we don't want to have to learn about the same kinds of dangers over and over again. But the downside is that sometimes the things that are imprinted in the amygdala's circuits are maladaptive.

In these instances, we pay dearly for the incredible efficiencies of the fear system. (p.252)

Stubborn determination is not intentional, but is an unconscious response to find safety. As the child develops cognitively over the years, the fear of being vulnerable may increase, reducing natural curiosity and exploration, which blocks the ability to be open to loving and trusting again. Nagging questions can haunt the child: *Why did my mother leave me? ... Why did my father not protect me? ... Why did my parents not keep me?*

Insecurity is often accompanied by an anxious belief that "It could happen again." Milder forms of the fear of abandonment may repeat when a person experiences any subsequent rejection while growing up. Even a slight failure at school or in a physical activity can reinforce a child's belief that he is unworthy, incapable, or incompetent: innately "bad." This "bad baby syndrome" feeling of unworthiness goes back to an initial loss in the child's life.

Close relationships feel scary when we don't trust the permanence of any relationship. To avoid this risk, a bereaved child may become controlling—reject others first, before he can be rejected. It takes courage to love again. It takes a secure sense of self.

'golden child'

Equally problematic is an adopted child who is told he was adopted because he was "special." If the child translates "special" as meaning "without flaws," he can become extremely sensitive to criticism, leading to feeling the need to be perfect in order to maintain the image of being special.

Young children's beliefs can be caught up in illogical thoughts, such as: *I have to be PERFECT or I will be gotten rid of. If I was abandoned once, it could happen again* (van Gulden and Bartels-Rabb 1999). Remember, feelings are not based in logic—but are founded in life's experiences and traumas.

> *When we challenge our fears, we defeat them. When we grapple with our difficulties, they lose their hold upon us. When we dare to face the things which scare us, we open the door to freedom.*—Author unknown

ANGER

and some things

Anger ranges from irritation to fury and rage. The physical effects are a faster heart rate, higher blood pressure, and increased adrenaline. Uncontrolled anger can manifest as aggression. When we feel provoked, threatened, vulnerable, or fragile, we get angry and may counter with a like disposition. We want to control *our* life, *our* destiny, *our* choices. We feel someone has stolen our right to happiness.

When we feel doom coming down upon us, everything feels narrow and tight, and we choke with the inability to reason. We have to do something! We have to solve it. We feel unsafe, which creates a sense of increased vulnerability. Assaults, prejudice, and violence are projected anger and, subsequently, rage.

"All good" and "all bad" attitudes are normal at the developmental ages from two to five. People and actions are either good or bad in that moment. Children do not see them as both. Their reasoning capability is not yet able to hold the good and bad at the same time. The child idealizes in "all or nothing" perceptions and judges experiences with "all or nothing" reasoning. A thwarted desire may be met with anger due to frustration. If the child grows in chronological age, but stays stuck emotionally at this anger level, he may collapse into tantrums and aggression whenever needs are not being satisfied. Not a pretty picture in an older person.

Rage nullifies creativity and the ability to move forward. Dwelling on grief, a lost award, a real failure to estimate a situation properly, a regret, or feeling unjustly treated, can disable the ability to manage today the tasks at hand with full attention and energy. Robert G. Ingersoll (1892) wrote that anger is a wind that "blows out the lamp of the mind."

When a child embraces a failure or owns up to a mistake, he has the freedom and space to create a new approach, which restores equilibrium and self-worth. In these times, he finds an inner core harmony and an ability to cope, without the burden of distress or self-chastisement. He accepts the circumstance and can put energy into finding a strategy that will allow going forward.

Moving forward is part of the process of the expansion of the child's emerging self, but it is hard to move forward in a state of anger. In a cartoon, Ziggy stated, "Instead of learning the real lessons of life, we miss them because we were too busy being frustrated and impatient."

Anger has a wholesome side. Helping children find a wholesome, productive outlet for their anger can empower them, and builds rewarding, constructive emotions. Anger can function as an incentive and energy to change things. Anger and injustice were the incentive for Mothers Against Drunk Driving (MADD). As Emerson wrote, "A good indignation brings out all one's power."

> *Holding on to anger is like grasping a hot coal with the intent of throwing it at someone else; you are the one who gets burned.*—Buddha

SHAME AND GUILT *each emerges in first wks of life.*

Part of feeling shame is feeling incomplete, and often follows a premature separation from the birth mother. As children become better able to judge their actions, empathy-through-attachment experiences expand to an awareness of a moral conscience. Shame in childhood sets social limits, teaching children to associate cause and effect. Cultural anthropologist Ruth Benedict (1934) described shame as a violation of social values, shame for thoughts and behaviors no one else knows about; and guilt as a violation of inner values, guilt to gain other people's approval.

earlier (Shame typically emerges in a personality at 18 months to three years) of age, when one is highly egocentric. Initially, shame is empathy, looking at our own actions in relation to others. Developing toddlers learn to stop their inappropriate behaviors and to adapt to others' responses—to regain approval of the loved one.

Shame (self-reproach) is early in developing a sense of self, and identifies feelings of disgrace for who one is. At ages one to three, how we sense who we are is based on "all or nothing" reasoning (e.g. "I'm a good boy," or "I'm a bad boy"), which is experienced at a deep visceral level, not conceptualized through words but experienced in the entire body. This is why shame is identified with feelings of disgrace.

A child who becomes stuck in shame is unable to move through grief and expands into "toxic shame" or self-judgment, believing "I'm all bad and you're all good" or "You're all bad and I'm all good." It is difficult for this child to perceive gray areas that allow for compassion and forgiveness of self and others. Toxic shame results in feelings of contempt, followed by bitter, critical judgment and rigidity in moral reasoning, and becomes pathological shame.

Toxic shame is a double-edged sword of self-contempt, not mere embarrassment or guilt. On one side, a deep sense of unworthiness causes the child to hide from himself any understanding or culpability of his thoughts and behaviors. Avoidance is achieved in two ways: totally distancing from the event (i.e. dissociation); recognizing the "bad" behavior and subsequent physical distress and distancing by refusing to take any responsibility for his actions (i.e. lying, blaming).

The function of both scenarios is to reduce the child's suffering. The other side of toxic shame is manifested when the child regresses and believes he must suffer in order to be forgiven. These children feel they must be condemned forever without reprieve and that they deserve to suffer for their transgressions. These children beat themselves up psychologically, and at times even physically through self-mutilation. Either side of shame is extremely damaging to a child developing a secure sense of self. When stuck at this level, the child is constantly trying to justify his actions rather than use intellect to manage emotions and behaviors productively.

Shame can be a motivator to change behavior during early years, or it can create a desire to hide any "less than" feelings from self and others. A client told me, "I *know* I did not cause my mother's death when I was three, but I always *felt* it was my fault."

Guilt is first felt at ages three to four, emerging from the earlier *earlier* developmental level of shame. Guilt is more discriminative. Guilt is for one's *behavior*, not one's entire self. We never hear someone say, "Guilt on you!" Even in a court of law, one is found guilty for an offense, not for one's core self.

With healthy guilt, a child feels remorseful and wants to change his/her behavior, make amends, reconnect, and repair the rupture. He is less judgmental and can more easily take responsibility for personal actions.

"Shame is closely related to guilt," wrote Paul Ekman (2001), "but there is a key qualitative difference." He explains:

> No audience is needed for feelings of guilt, no one else need know, for the guilty person is his own judge. Not so for shame. The

humiliation of shame requires disapproval or ridicule by others. If no one ever learns of a misdeed there will be no shame, but there still might be guilt. Of course, there may be both. The distinction between shame and guilt is very important, since these two emotions may tear a person in opposite directions. The wish to relieve guilt may motivate a confession, but the wish to avoid the humiliation of shame may prevent it. (p.65–66)

In adoptions, shame in later years is often experienced as feeling "not good enough to keep." The child worries that the new caregivers will also abandon him. The child feels defective, fragmented. This is why it is so important when a young child begins to think about being "given up" by the biological parents (around age six) that these thoughts be discussed openly and honestly. (For further information, see Chapter 8.) The roots of these feelings are summed up very concisely in the quotation below.

> The difference between guilt and shame is very clear—in
> theory. We feel guilty for what we do. We feel shame for what
> we are.—Lewis B. Smedes

DEPRESSION

The downside of depression is anger turned inward. The symptoms can manifest as pessimism, feeling inadequate, a despondent lack of activity; ongoing sadness, despair, loss of energy and difficulty in dealing with daily life; feeling worthless and hopeless, a loss of pleasure in activities, changes in eating or sleeping habits, and thoughts of death or suicide.

If not addressed, depressed children can relinquish their inner search to recover what they have lost and see their dreams as impossible to put back together. In this fragile, vulnerable state, they can then dive into deeper states of despair, helplessness, and hopelessness. They can't imagine a future, and they no longer look forward with hope. This is *maladaptive* depression.

Depressed children may cry inconsolably, curl into a fetal position, or hang limp. Sad crying is different from rage or terror crying; which are indicated by a stiff, tense body, protruding blood vessels, a shrill voice, perhaps a few tears. For very young children, rage crying is described by

John Bowlby (1981) as "Protest and Despair." *Protest* is the attempt to regain the presence of the person; *despair* is the realization that he has been unsuccessful. When children sustain a significant loss, they question their competency and value: *How weak am I if I can't turn this around?* When a child moves through developmental transitions in the grief journey, such behavior is typical.

The upside of depression, said Ken Moses, is that it's the medium by which a child can move to higher functioning. This can be a turning point in the grief process. With a significant loss early in life, each developmental stage motivates redefining a loss cognitively, emotionally, and socially. The redefinition moves the child to a higher level of competency, value, and power in handling life's tragedies. The child begins to move through deep feelings and to accept that he will be okay even with the absence of the loved one. The ability to deal with deep emotions brings a new sense of courage and an expanding strong, core self.

With depressed children, listen and observe carefully. Stay with them through their pain and they will learn how to sustain through their own pain during their later life losses. Rollo May encapsulates the stultifying effect of depression in children:

Depression is the inability to construct a future.

WITHDRAWAL, INDIFFERENCE, AND DESPAIR

Withdrawal, indifference, and despair are coping mechanisms for when children feel powerless. They exhibit eye avoidance, avert their gaze, and lack facial expression. During extreme loss, they sit or lie limp or curl into a fetal position. Withdrawal allows bereaved children time to regroup, to begin to deal with external change.

Intense despair, or severe withdrawal beyond a few weeks, or a lack of response to nurturing interventions, indicate that professional help is needed. It takes a healthy, compassionate adult to "mirror and gaze" a depressed child. Developmental studies had revealed that a caregiver's gaze is a critical regulator of arousal in infant–mother interactions (Brazelton, Koslowski, and Main 1974; Stern 1974). The caregiver's face reflects back the infant (child's) feeling state allowing what Siegel (1999) defined as "feeling felt." It is a mutual interaction of understanding, one to another, offering a "safe space" for the child to experience and contain (i.e. regulate) the feeling sensations in that moment. Attuned mirroring and gazing requires the sensitivity of the caregiver to his/her infant (child) to monitor and maintain the interaction based on the infant's capacity for attention and need for withdrawal, modulating, and regulating this interdependent communication dance. According to Hofer (1984), gaze patterns may be active "hidden regulators" of arousal throughout one's lifespan. The adult must be able to be fully present with the child, emotionally holding him or her through the suffering—not rushing or trying to divert the process to avoid feelings.

if it comes at all

FULLY ACCEPTING a childhood loss does not come until the mid twenties when we are able to view life abstractly. Until then, a bereaved individual continues adjusting to the loss through each developmental level.

The above-described range of emotions recurs over and over throughout the developmental years. Some stages are easier, some harder. Periods of acceptance and regrouping are intermittent and usually pertain to select aspects of a child's life. When a child is able to regroup, he is open to replacing shattered dreams with new dreams.

CHAPTER 4

THE STAGES OF GRIEF

The best and most beautiful things in this world cannot be seen or even heard, but must be felt with the heart.—Helen Keller

The grief process appears to have two distinct stages and multiple, interconnecting phases. Waves of distress come in two main forms: acute and chronic (i.e. slowly developing in the background). Both forms reflect a struggle of ego identity (Hofer 1984). Ego identity, simply put, is the relationship one has to oneself, as distinct from the world and others. Although specific definitions vary, one's personal self-identity is developed over time from the very early years into late adolescence and comprises the foundational experiences and interactions with others in their environment. Out of these experiences emerges one's beliefs about oneself and one's world. Early grief can significantly affect how one perceives oneself and thereby influence one's attachments and behavioral interactions with others throughout one's lifespan.

Visceral impulses and emotional experiences underlie all mental activity. Extreme, chronic sorrow destroys the capacity for joy and can render children indifferent (Shand 1914). They may even feel immobilized. It is crucial to address children's grief process, because an early loss can shift their expectations, influence them neurologically, psychologically and physically, and predispose them to disease and stress later in life.

STAGE I: SHOCK AND NUMBNESS

No one reacts to significant loss in exactly the same way, yet there are several common reactions. Shock and numbness are automatic physiological responses to intense feelings and thoughts brought on by the initial stress of a loss. These responses also occur at various developmental stages during lifestyle transitions as well as in creative problem-solving phases of life.

Shock and numbness can last anywhere from a few seconds or minutes to several hours or weeks. Shock functions as a protection against being overwhelmed by emotion, which allows the body and mind to shut down at the same time, because if the mind is "out-to-lunch" the body is like a car without a driver. Shock keeps the body from total fragmentation. When a child is overwhelmed, the breaker (i.e. parasympathetic nervous system) abruptly shuts down the mind and body. This is akin to shutting down the engine of a car when it becomes overheated. Just as the engine won't explode, the body won't collapse from an abrupt burst of tragedy. Shock buys the body time to absorb a trauma, so the body may gradually reawaken with the mind.

During shock and numbness, a child may feel cold and clammy; may tremble, twitch, perspire, or be dizzy, or look dazed. A child may experience an episode of shock by "numbing out" emotionally and physically. An older child may faint, hurt in the chest, feel "choked up."

Shock is a form of *dissociation* (see Glossary). The child is unaware of what is going on inside and around her. Shock can be benign. Mark Twain wrote in his autobiography, upon hearing of the death of his daughter Susy:

> It is one of the mysteries of our nature that a man, all unprepared, can receive a thunderstroke like that and live. There is but one reasonable explanation of it. The intellect is stunned by the shock and but gropingly gathers the meaning of the words. The power to realize their full import is mercifully wanting. (quoted in Moffat 1992)

Mark Twain's words fit eloquently into the journey of developmental grief. Although he was not referring to childhood grief when he wrote, "It will be years before the tale of lost essentials is complete, and not till then can he truly know the magnitude of his disaster" (quoted in Moffat 1992).

At each developmental stage, new ways of viewing a loss bring new questions. The experience of shock is the beginning of reworking the earlier loss. When the mind and body begin to awaken, the child moves into denial.

STAGE II: DENIAL

In China on Mother's Day, a red rose is given to a living mother; if the mother has died, a white rose is given to the living children to honor their mothers. In America for Mother's Day, cards, flowers, and presents are sent only to the living mother. Motherless children and adults are left with memories of loss. Denial buys the bereaved child time to develop inner strength and resources to cope with their experiences and the information they have received.

Denial and disbelief limit how much reality one is ready to face (van Gulden and Bartells-Robb 1999). Denial involves a choice (subconscious or conscious) not to accept the reality of a loss. Disbelief (shock and numbness) blocks much of the truth. Denial is normal when emerging from Stage 1: Shock.

A child who faces a loss head-on may plunge into despair, which may erupt into tantrums and/or dissociation. Denial allows the child to block the flood of thoughts, visceral feelings, and emotions until she can tolerate them (van Gulden and Bartells-Robb 1999). A child's cognitive development is a natural filter that allows time, through each developmental stage, to conceptualize how and why a loss occurred.

A young child who has to address a loss at full impact may collapse from a lack of defense mechanisms and become stuck; inner strength and the experience necessary to negotiate the grief journey have not yet been developed. When a loss occurs before one can speak, the experience is forever and indelibly imprinted in the implicit (unconscious) memory (see Glossary).

At each developmental stage, a child is reminded of the lost loved one and the hopes and expectations that have been shattered. This is often experienced while witnessing others of the same age having experiences the child no longer can. At each stage, the child watches others access what she has lost. One woman who had lost her mother when she was a toddler told me, every Mother's Day in Puerto Rico, her aunt and grandmother would make her "wear a pink rose," symbolic in that country that her mother had died. She hated Mother's Day.

"I hated to wear it," she stated, her voice cracking with the painful memory, a concrete demonstration of how different she was from the other children. "It was always a reminder of how much I missed my mother," how much life had changed without her. Every year, the pink rose triggered the reality that her dream was shattered. As a child, wearing the pink rose had not been comforting. It had been heartrending.

A compassionate adult must be available to take a child's hand and walk the grief journey with her until early adulthood. Develop the art of acknowledging and discussing the child's "good, bad, and ugly" thoughts and feeling, which gives the child the opportunity to learn and practice the intimate arts of communication and acceptance.

In Dr. Ken Moses' seminar I attended in 1984, he identified four phases of denial: Denial of Facts; Denial of Comprehension of Facts; Denial of Implications/Structural Changes; Denial of Emotional States. In addressing the phases of denial to fit developmental grief, I have changed some of his terminology and definitions.

Phase 1: Denying the facts of a loss or a death

"It didn't happen."

"She was just here."

"My dad is coming home. He's just on a long trip."

"Mommy's sick and had to go to the hospital, but she'll be better soon."

"My parents aren't getting a divorce. Daddy isn't moving far away."

"You are my mom and dad. I was *not* adopted."

"My mommy's dead. We have to be quiet, because she is sleeping. She'll come home when she wakes up."

Denial of the facts is typical of all of us when first exposed to something we are not ready to handle. The zero to two-year-old physically experiences the facts of a significant loss, because of the abrupt removal of the hidden regulators, which causes the child's body to become dysregulated. The body remembers even when the child lacks the explicit memory (verbal memory of events, see Glossary) that has yet to emerge.

Toddlers and preschoolers experience loss with a sense of "magical thinking," because they cannot yet understand the idea of permanence. They can state the fact (e.g. "Mommy is dead. I am adopted."); however, the realization of what these words really mean (*comprehension of the fact*) must wait for later years. Nevertheless, denial of the facts doesn't usually last long, no matter how old the child is. Reality sets in, because every day the person (pet or home) is no longer there.

> "Mommy is no longer cooking the meals, cleaning the house, doing the laundry. Taking me to music lessons … Holding me when I'm frightened … Mending my scraps and bruises."

> "Dad doesn't play rough and tumble with me. He's not at my baseball games to watch me, pat me on the back, holler in celebration of my hits. Our fishing trips are gone."

Denial of the facts is tested when a child's home changes, whether due to finances, support adjustment, or increased time at a daycare or a relative's home. A surviving or remaining parent often has increased demands; or the child may have to be moved to Grandma's because Mom or Dad is away on military duty, in the hospital for a major illness, or the single parent's job requires extensive time away on business.

If the loss is a pet, it is not recommended to "collude" in the child's denial by replacing the pet secretly overnight as if it is the same pet. Children sense the difference no matter what you tell them. Such deceit creates confusion and mistrust.

Phase 2: Difficulty comprehending what has happened

A four-year-old girl loses her mother. "Mother was very, very sick. She died, but she can return." In the French movie *Ponette*, a young mother dies in a car accident. The daughter tells the father, "There are holes in the ground which might allow her to return sometime."

A ten-year-old boy loses his mother. "Mommy got hurt in a car crash. She was so broken that her heart stopped and she died." He recognizes that Mommy will not return. He understands the permanence of the loss and the concrete facts surrounding the loss. For him, the deeper *whys* will have to wait to be understood.

At age fifteen, the boy can better comprehend the car accident. "Mother was driving drunk … Hit by a drunk driver … Working long shifts and fell asleep at the wheel." An adolescent is able to look at a loss through the lens of abstract reasoning, which enables her to ascertain a broader perspective of causes and effects. She is able to see what led up to the death, the facts surrounding the death, and begin to problem-solve some of the potential consequences as a result of the loss.

At age twenty-five. A young man's mother died when he was three months old. No one in his family filled in the details until he was eight. As a young adult, he is critically missing an essential piece of his puzzle, because his preverbal, implicit memories left him with a nebulous (yet accurate) sense of something missing. Until someone shares some of the details of the missing puzzle piece, he will remain in this murky state of loss in a realm of knowing, yet not knowing.

AT THE EARLY LEVEL of comprehension of the facts in the grief process, a bereaved child may acknowledge the fact of a loss. In so doing, she can become highly anxious as to who will now be available to care for him or her. Adapting to another person's rhythm and style can be extremely fatiguing. Comprehension of a loss evolves over time with children as they develop more cognitive skills, insight, and experiences. Some insights bring comfort; however, some can increase suffering, because they may throw the child back into the earlier stage of "shock and numbness." When a loss occurs at an early age, the developmental journey through grief takes years genuinely to understand all of the elements of what was lost, so that the mind, body, and spirit will have time to absorb and comprehend the loss.

Any loss has many ramifications. When it is the caregiver (e.g. parent) who was an integral part of the child's daily life, the devastation is felt each time she comes into contact with the routines. For the new care-

---

To comprehend a loss, a child often reads storybooks about her type of loss, watches movies (fit for her cognitive level), searches the internet (late elementary and up); talks with friends, relatives, professionals, and others who have had a similar loss.

Many children's stories portray the children journeying through life after a significant loss. The fairy tales *Bambi*, *Cinderella*, *Snow White*, and *The Little Mermaid*; the Brothers Grimms' fairy tale *Hansel and Gretel*, religious stories like that of Moses, and movies like *Pollyanna* and *The Secret Garden* offer insight into children's unique experiences and perspective. A number of well-known books have featured orphans: Charles Dickens' *Oliver Twist*, Mark Twain's *Tom Sawyer*, J.K. Rowling's *Harry Potter*, Harold Gray's *Little Orphan Annie*, and the Baudelaire siblings in the *Series of Unfortunate Events* by Daniel Handler under the pseudonym Lemony Snicket. The characters are self-contained and introspective, and strive in various ways to recapture affection. Supportive parents being absent from the scenes makes the characters' difficulties even more severe. Orphans metaphorically search through "shadows of loss" for self-understanding in an attempt to find their roots…or identity.

givers, identifying the lost hidden regulators that kept the child in a state of physiological balance is part of comprehending the facts.

Grownups often fail to understand children's grief—because we don't remember or fully understand how they grieve. Children cannot explain in words how they are feeling. When a loss occurs in a child's life before she has learned words, there is no explicit memory within which to "park" the experience. For example, a child adopted as an infant or toddler (i.e. preverbal) lacks both the conscious (explicit) memory to park previous experiences and the language to express feelings. Prior to age five or six, a young adopted child understands her adoption story from very concrete facts: *I was born in this mommy's belly, and then came to live with Mommy and Daddy* or *I lived in China until two. Then Mommy and Daddy came and took me home.* This thinking is a form of addition, but when higher cognitive thinking begins, the realization of subtraction arises. *To get to you, someone had to give me up.* This new fact tends to be followed by: *There must have been something wrong with me.* Such ideas never arose in the child's mind before this. But you can be an ally and source of support to a grieving child through telling stories, which offers opportunities for the child to place herself within the story and supports the quest to refind stability, identity, and belonging.

At each new cognitive stage, as children's ability to comprehend increases, new information and questions arise. So, if the child has the courage to ask, have the respect to answer her questions. Denying an answer can break a child's trust in you. If you don't know the answer, it's fair to say so. If you have a way to help her find an answer, join the child in searching for the answer. Doing so will strengthen your relationship, while helping to build the child's inner strength and tolerance for dealing with painful experiences, tough questions, and information as an adult.

It is essential to watch for changes in the child's mood and behavior, and to discuss any questions—at a level appropriate to her developmental stage. Too much information can be overwhelming; too little is dismissive and leaves the child to fantasize the answers. The Pebble Technique by van Gulden and Bartels-Rabb described on pp.101–103 is a way to "test the waters" of a child's thoughts and feelings.

Staying stuck in grief is resisting the need to ask relevant questions. Once a child asks a form of the question, "What did I lose?" she has begun the conscious exploration of the healing journey. The question is a form of the shattered dream described in Chapter 1. The emerging answers can help the child to move through that level.

Phase 3: Denying the need to change routines, schedules, behaviors, beliefs

At this phase of denial, grief-ridden children deny that a loss has changed their daily life, or they may deny some of the implications a loss means to them. They don't want to do anything in a different way. They don't want their life structure to change. This can be an attempt to hold onto the past and the loved one. If the child and adults have insufficiently addressed Phases 1 and 2 (physical, cognitive, social/emotional), she may be inconsistent and unclear in *what* needs to change, as well as *how* best to adapt to change in a wholesome manner. In addition, the motivation to do things differently may be inadequate to maintain healthy, responsible responses.

A death changes life's daily rhythm. It can take several people to share the responsibilities once filled by a lost loved one: cooking, grocery shopping, cleaning, laundry, car pool, medical appointments, sports/cultural activities and lessons, rising and bedtime rituals, playtime and exploration opportunities. The key is to plan and implement who will pick up the lost hidden regulators embedded in the child's activities. The method is to define who will do what, when, where, how. The Puzzle Technique (see pp.144–147) is one way to identify and begin this process.

Adults who don't see the implications of a child's loss may themselves be stuck in one or more of the four phases of denial, originating from their own unresolved past loss. Therapists, medical professionals, and educators also need to spend time helping these adults to understand what such a loss means, for themselves as well as their children. If the adult is stuck in the grief process, it is highly likely the child will remain stuck as well. Children take their cues from their caregivers.

To reduce bereaved children's sense of anxiety and vulnerability, allow them to have an active role in what is happening in their lives. If life is to change for bereaved children, they need a say in how this will happen for them. Empowering children during a time of vulnerability defuses their resistance to changes in routine and gives them choices (ages two and up).

Explore bereaved children's shattered dreams with them. Once you know what was lost, it's easier to problem-solve and negotiate how some of the loss essentials might be replaced. This supports the children in changing their rituals, activities, and routines.

Phase 4: Buried and unfamiliar emotions

Anticipate that any bereaved child needs calming, so she won't be over-whelmed with thoughts and feelings about life, that it can destroy randomly and without warning. A loss throws children into confusion. Their sense of self is disrupted. They may regress to an earlier level of development and temporarily lose skills achieved, because the earlier behavior is familiar and feels safer and more comfortable.

We all have some emotions that are more comfortable for us than others. The ones we rarely experience are the ones we may not even acknowledge to ourselves. These are the ones others never see expressed on our face, in our words or behaviors. Such emotions are not intention-ally repressed; they are the ones to which we have had, as a child or adolescent, minimal exposure and experience within our environ-ment and social system. The emotions are "underdeveloped" and "underutilized" because they are unfamiliar. Over time, this can lead to avoidance and increased vulnerability when life necessitates dealing with the buried emotions in order for us to have a successful resolution of conflict, including going through the grief process.

People only deny unfamiliar emotions, ones they have had little opportunity and support to experience and express. Girls often feel more comfortable showing fear and depression, but not anger or aggression. Boys are often more comfortable expressing anger, rather than fear or depression. Western culture, as well as male and female biology, also play a role in determining which behaviors are most often expressed, versus those that are hidden, even from ourselves.

Blocking feelings, however, can keep us stuck in the past and unable to move forward. A child who experiences trauma early in life and doesn't have external supports or a secure base may suffer pathological mourning (see Glossary) and is more at risk of dissociation (especially overwhelming emotions) in the future.

To find resolution, we must learn to handle our undesirable emotions and thoughts, such as sadness or depression. "No use crying over spilt milk" is an old saying. So is, "Life must go on. Grin and bear it." However, such attitudes restrict the grief process to only surface (superficial) emotions.

It is important to be gentle with the process, digesting foreign feelings in small doses, allowing time to become familiar with more fragile feelings as well as ways to handle them. The developmental journey through grief, due to the stages of increasing capacity, affords a child the time and experience to do just that—*if* a supportive adult is available.

Caregivers, therapists, educators, and medical staff can support building a child's inner strength and provide the resources for coping with emotions that flood periodically during the grief journey. Knowing the age-related developmental phases helps in understanding how to support a child's needs at any and every age.

Emotions are natural and essential to be healthy cognitively, socially, and physically. Being able to express deep loss genuinely releases confusion and emboldens the child's inner strength to face his or her new life.

PART II

GRIEF THROUGH THE AGES

Photo by John Schoenwalter

CHAPTER 5

INTRODUCTION: GRIEF AND DEVELOPMENTAL STAGES

Dreams are renewable. No matter what our age or condition, there are still untapped possibilities within us and new beauty waiting to be born.—Dale Turner

Once it was believed that infants, toddlers, and preschoolers do not grieve an early loss. Nothing could be further from the truth!

> The dialogue between the child and a living partner has to precede not only all meaningful relations with the animate, but also all imaginary exchanges with the inanimate... Man, when he is deprived of the dialogue from infancy, turns into an empty asocial husk, spiritually dead, as a candidate for custodial care... Life, as we conceive of it, is achieved through the dialogue (Spitz 1963, p.159).

All children, from infants to adolescents, need a developmentally appropriate and supportive environment that allows them to master tasks crucial to each life stage: physically, emotionally, psychologically, socially, morally. Failure at any stage can lead to great difficulties later in life (Havighurst and DeHann 1957). A solid understanding of this age-related, neuropsychological grief process is helpful for intervening with any child or young adult who has experienced a significant loss.

Thoughts of death occur at an early age. Significant loss causes a child to feel less "at home" because the pattern of daily life has been disrupted. The hidden regulators (wrapped in familiar routines with the lost loved one) are acutely and chronically missed when they are abruptly and permanently removed. Children are vulnerable to the neglect of their needs, especially if the adults are overwhelmed and unavailable to support them through the grief process.

Coping involves the interplay with what is coming into alignment at each age, as well as tending to the grief process of losing a significant other. Lack of experience with loss, or a history of ineffective coping, makes children more vulnerable in ways adults are not. Past losses can complicate a new loss, adding to a child's levels of stress and separation anxiety; and he is vulnerable to increased feelings of insecurity, distrust, abandonment, and alienation. Coping strategies may be restricted by narrower life experiences, immature cognitive processing, and shorter attention span. As children develop, more sophisticated coping skills emerge for experiential practice opportunities, supported by expanding concentration and attention.

Brain development causes maturation in thinking ability, behavior, emotional regulation, and social capacity, allowing children gradually to absorb a life loss through the years. Children progress developmentally through awareness of death. If they are caught by a loss in an early developmental stage, they are vulnerable to revisiting their initial loss when they are in each new stage. Ineffective grieving early on can negatively impact development and complicate their progress to maturity.

Abilities just developing, or not yet emerged, are the most sensitive and most often disrupted by a loss. Theories surrounding childhood losses have undergone changes in perception, in a similar way to post-traumatic stress disorder (PTSD) and traumatic brain injury (TBI). Children had been thought to be more resilient and their ability to experience the depths of mourning less intense. Erroneous conclusions were made, suggesting it was better to have a trauma, brain injury or loss at a younger age due to children's (assumed) ability to recover neuropsychologically, emotionally, and cognitively.

Recent research, however, consistently has reported that pediatric brain injury, post-traumatic stress, and early loss actually are more devastating. Research has confirmed changes that can occur in the brain on a cellular level and result in altered pathway conduction, abnormal changes in hormones and neurotransmitters, lower immune-system response, and the risk of permanently altered brain function. It has been discovered that such changes can affect a child's functioning for life, culminating in substantial vulnerability that can increase with aging (Hofer 1996; Houston and Warnock 1999; Meany 2001; Scaer 2005; Schore 1994; van der Kolk *et al.* 2006; Ylvisaker 1998).

Children and adolescents do not grieve in isolation. They grieve within the social context of their family, friends, peers, cultural setting, and community. They often mirror the coping and communication styles modeled by the adults around them, and they may constrain their own emotions. Children need to be perceived as legitimate mourners, not disenfranchised from their grief. But don't forget that children may be anxious about the basic necessities of life: food and shelter, and that they cannot allow and feel their grief until their basic needs are assured.

Creating goals for dealing with grief and moving forward is important. This begins first with external support, but gradually, it will be incorporated as a skill the child can self-initiate.

Later events can trigger renewed grieving: holidays, birthdays, and major transitions, such as entering school and graduation; the onset of puberty; first dates; important successes or failures; career selections; marriage; birth of the first child. Children and adolescents often re-grieve at a later time—when they have a more mature perspective. A bereaved child moving through later developmental stages changes the context for understanding an earlier loss, and for coming to terms with its impact. A critical developmental task here is learning to trust others; disruption can induce severe or long-lasting anxiety and compromise future relationships.

Children shift between grief and engagement, dealing with loss, then adapting, while coping with their many new responsibilities (Stroebe and Schut 1999). However, as a bereaved child gets older, he may find maladaptive ways to diminish suffering (e.g. drugs, alcohol, sex, self-mutilation, high-risk sports, truancy, dropping out of school).

A surviving child may experience survivor guilt, which can lead to estrangement of friends, a secondary loss. The surviving child might be troubled by a longing to complete unfinished but anticipated shared experiences and aspirations. In addition, survivor guilt can, if not addressed, keep the child stuck in the grief journey, believing he deserves to suffer. Survivor guilt, as a result, can lead to toxic shame if left unattended.

Other people's lack of tolerance for a child's grief, and insensitive responses from peers, cause a bereaved child or adolescent to feel vulnerable. Feeling different or estranged, he may withdraw, avoid others, or respond abruptly.

Many reactions in a bereaved child are prevalent during the months immediately following the death of a loved one or other significant change, such as an adoption or divorce. Although some effects may not appear until years later (due to maturational reasons), most behavioral changes show up within two years. By the beginning of the second year into the loss, there is a marked difference in how bereaved children see themselves in terms of school performance, general behavioral conduct, and overall self-esteem. Worden and Silverman (1996) found higher levels of withdrawal, anxiety, and social problems at the two-year mark, as well as lower levels of self-esteem and self-efficacy. A significant percentage (21%) showed serious problems in handling their loss.

Most children exhibit some grief responses, yet seldom all of them. The intensity of their reactions to a loss and its duration varies with each child and is influenced by their age, ability to anticipate loss, understanding the concepts of permanence and death, reaction of the surviving caregivers, and quality of their relationship with the person who died or left.

Normal grief in children is experienced physically, emotionally, behaviorally, and neurologically. Some examples are provided below:

- *Physically:* They may experience sleep difficulty (e.g. sleep too long, difficulty falling asleep, waking in the middle of the night, nightmares or night terrors, trouble getting back to sleep, difficulty getting up in the morning); bedwetting, headaches, stomach aches, appetite changes (e.g. stuffing to fill the emptiness, nausea when eating, lack of appetite); constipation, diarrhea; extreme fatigue, extreme restlessness.

- *Emotionally:* Separation anxiety, fear of others dying or leaving, school phobias, shame, guilt, anger, illusions/hallucinations, helplessness, hopelessness, fear of being kidnapped, generalized anxiety, learning difficulty, death fantasy, suicidal thoughts in the hope of reuniting with the lost loved one.

- *Behaviorally:* Regression to an earlier stage where the child felt safer and secure, irritation, agitation, explosive outbursts, increased temper tantrums, overdependence, clinging to the new caregiver, reluctance to explore, diminished curiosity, shortened concentration, hyperactive/hypoactive, hypervigilance/hypovigilance.

- *Neurologically:* Loss can influence whatever is coming into alignment in the brain. The critical periods and sensitive periods (see Chapter 1) are most at risk of being compromised in a child's neurological development. Remember Hebb's (1949) theory, "Use it or Lose it."

Butterflies mirror the normal psychological development from birth. From the mother's womb until the child emerges as an independent adult in the mid-twenties, he is in the cocoon stage of life, incubating his life potential. The hidden regulators and familiar identifications started while in the womb allow the child immediately to connect with the mother when leaving the womb. During the first 25 years, a child's interdependence is like being in a cocoon, because he is still developing a personal identity in order to be able to "fly" on his own. The aspects of children's shattered dreams change over the years:

Three years old: "How I wish it was Mommy taking me to my first day of preschool."

Eight years old: "I wish Dad was here for my games. He would be proud of me."

Twelve-year-old female starting menstruation: "If only Mom was here. She would know how to stop this pain and teach me what to do."

High-school graduation day: "I wish my dad could see me in my cap and gown. I am the first in our family to graduate. This was his dream for me."

Young woman on her wedding day: "Dad, I always dreamed it would be your arm I would be holding as I walked down the aisle. It would be you telling me how beautiful I am today."

New mother: "Mom, this is your first granddaughter. I so wanted you to hold her, and for her to get to know how wonderful you were. I miss not being able to talk to you about parenting advice."

With each developmental stage from birth to the mid-twenties, a child's ability to adapt and comprehend expands, allowing a loss to be absorbed in a broader perspective. The following Buddhist metaphor describes the developmental stages of losing a loved one:

> *If a tablespoon of salt is added to a cup of water, the water tastes strongly of the salt. If a tablespoon of salt is added to a jug of water, it tastes less salty. If the salt is added to a pond, the taste is further dissipated.*

CHAPTER 6

BIRTH TO TODDLER
(AGES 0 TO 2)

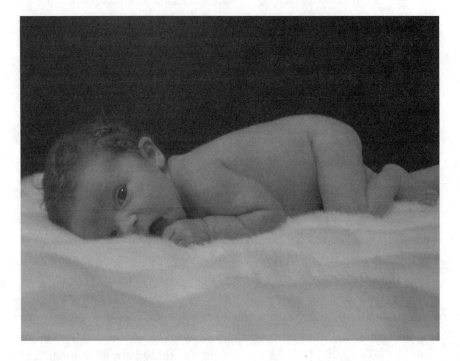

Photo by Brenna Aschermann

MARNIE'S STORY: EARLY SEPARATION

Marnie was born with medical complications requiring a seven-week hospital stay in the pediatric intensive care unit (ICU), a busy place all day and night; with smells of alcohol, antiseptic soaps and lotions, medications, bodily fluids, milk formulas.

Even at night, lights were usually on due to the continual activity of nurses. It was never a quiet place, with sounds of unfamiliar voices, breathing machines, footsteps, medical machines being moved, phones ringing, the sounds of various instruments and machines that monitor the infants' functioning; plus custodial cleaning and babies wailing in pain, fear, hunger, and discomfort.

Touch was not always gentle or comforting or warm, but was fraught with pain due to the needles, intravenous tubes, cold clamps, rubber gloves touching the skin, and being held down to perform the painful daily procedures for Marnie's survival.

Her little body was never in a state of peace. She was more familiar with pain than comfort, daily changes than routine. Experiences such as hers were described by psychiatrist Robert Scaer (2005) in his book *The Trauma Spectrum*:

> As a society, we treat our infants with considerable nonchalance… medical science dogma that suggests that the preverbal infant is a nonsentient bundle of primitive reflexes…beliefs pronounced by self-proclaimed experts such as pediatricians or child psychologists who viewed the infant as impervious to pain and to the effect of a traumatic experience… Thus infants were exposed to many surgical and medical procedures without anesthetic and immobilized by paralytic agents. (pp.99–101)

Although there are many good pediatric units in hospitals today, Marnie was not a patient in one of these. Such incidents are not only in the past. Even today, they still occur in some pediatric ICUs during a child's very early, preverbal, years. I was sadly informed by several parents in my national seminars that this practice continues today. Many parents are told to leave their child's room so as not to interfere with the staff's ability to work "efficiently." In large cities, many of these parents immediately transferred their young child to a more compassionate hospital environment.

Marnie had no conscious (i.e. verbal) memories of those weeks. Nevertheless, she bore the burden of post-traumatic stress disorder (see van der Kolk *et al.* 2006). Her body (and limbic system: see Glossary) took the hit, where many of these early memories reside.

Now at age nine, she has accurate implicit memories (not in language but visceral feelings and images). When stressed about school or an impending activity, positive or negative (high anticipation of pleasure and displeasure triggered in the sympathetic nervous system), late at night she can't sleep and turns on all the lights in her room, along with the television, and plays fast-paced video games on her computer. Under extreme stress, she reverts to her time in the ICU, a busy, hectic atmosphere where she originally learned to sleep. Many of these early stimuli are now "hardwired from her early developing infant's system."

Marnie's parents were emotionally and physically available to her day and night—until they were told to leave her room. They gently stroked and patted her and spoke endearingly to her while she was in the incubator. When allowed out of the incubator, they held her and rocked her, wrapped in a receiving blanket that held their scent, told her stories and sang to her.

They were with her throughout the procedures; her pain was their pain. They held the suffering together with love and compassion. Their availability kept several of Marnie's hidden regulators in place, at least partially (i.e. through the familiarity of her parents' scents, voices, heartbeats, and visual contact via mirroring and gazing time). A nurse in my seminar described such experiences profoundly when she told the audience:

> As a young child, I had to undergo long and painful procedures. At that time in hospitals, parents were not allowed in the room. But I remembered seeing the faces of my mother and father glued to the glass window, watching me, holding me in their gaze. I never felt alone during this time. Indeed, *I could feel their love.* For me, knowing at a deep level that I was loved allowed me to endure my hospital stay.

Research studies suggest that a "good enough" caregiver's presence can maintain an infant's physiological system even in a fragile state, helping her resist total deterioration. The daily presence and interaction of Marnie's parents facilitated her development of a wholesome attaching relationship.

Nurses working in pediatric ICUs have told me about talking with these children and their families. Many parents are told by the doctors to go home, when they do not expect the baby to survive, believing it is better to save the parents the agony of attaching to their baby which will only intensify their grief when she dies.

Doctors can only guess what might happen. They do not know for sure.

Infants expected to die often survive. The ICU nurses see these children in the community years later and, as they get older, they hear of their progress through medical friends. They report that children whose parents are available during the insufferable days appear to do much better than the ones whose parents stay away. The supported children are better regulated affectively and behaviorally; whereas, the others are often out of control, hyperactive, and less attached to their parents.

Effects of early trauma

Early trauma includes loss, significant illness, abuse, and neglect. It can result in permanent alterations in the limbic area of the midbrain, an area critical to the development of the regulation of emotion. Early defenses take shape at all levels of the nervous system and become encoded in the entire being, and are like the air we breathe, utterly invisible (Reich 1945). Trauma in childhood without a caregiver intervening in a mindful manner arrests development; whereas, trauma in adulthood leads to regression (Krystal *et al.* 1998). These early years are absolutely critical in the building of a healthy emotional and physical foundation.

In the course of a long-term study of infant behavior in a nursery, Rene Spitz and his research assistant, Katherine Wolf, observed 123 orphaned infants for 12 to 18 months, during which time they encountered a striking syndrome (Spitz 1945a, 1945b). In the second half of the first year, a few of the infants developed a weepy behavior, in marked contrast to their previously happy and outgoing behavior. After a time, the weepiness gave way to withdrawal. The children would lie in their cots with averted faces, refusing to take part in the life around them. When approached, they ignored the observers. Some of them lost weight (instead of gaining), some suffered insomnia, all showed increased susceptibility to colds and eczema; and they all gradually declined in their cognitive, physical, and emotional abilities.

This behavior lasted three months. Then the weepiness subsided and it would only occur with strong provocation. In its place, frozen rigidity in expression appeared. They would lie or sit with wide-open, expressionless eyes; frozen, immobile faces; and a faraway look as if in a daze, often unaware of their environment. Communication with these children became increasingly difficult and finally impossible. They had shut down and shut off from their world.

These symptoms were not necessarily present at the same time, but most showed up at one point or another: apprehension, sadness, weepiness; lack of contact, rejection of environment, withdrawal; retardation of development and reaction to stimuli, slowness of movement, dejection, stupor; loss of appetite, refusal to eat, weight loss; and sleep disturbances.

This syndrome is similar to the classical descriptions of mourning, pathological mourning, and melancholia as written by Freud (1917) and by Karl Abraham (1912). The factor of decisive significance is the loss of the love object, the mother. They described an inward conflict among fear, guilt, and compulsive anger, with an outward expression of hostility.

HENRY'S STORY: LOSS IN THE SECOND YEAR

Henry was a busy, curious 18-month-old, the "light in his mother's eyes." His mother woke one sunny autumn morning with flu-like symptoms. By late morning, she was taken by ambulance to a hospital emergency room…where she died of a heart attack. She had been young, strong, and healthy. No one could have predicted this. No one was prepared.

Henry's dad had often worked late at his job while Mom was the constant in Henry's life. As parents, they had agreed she would be a stay-at-home mom for Henry's first three years of life, even though it meant his dad would put in longer hours to meet their financial obligations.

Prior to his mother's death, Henry was thrilled when she would play exploratory games with him; and take him to Jamboree to roll, slide, and tumble on the sensory-motor equipment with his friends. His days were filled with routines and familiar toys, mealtimes, naptimes, cuddle times, bath play, and his frequent check-backs on Mom to make sure she was still there while he played and explored his world with avid curiosity and

energy (see Mahler *et al.* 1975). Mom's secure presence during his explo-
rations provided him with encouragement and trust in his unfolding
developmental life skills, a time when independence collides with
dependency needs: the *Come here. Go away* phase. *No, I want to do this by
myself…BUT I want you to help me.*

And so Henry's ability to play by himself increased, as did his abilities to delay gratification, decrease impulsivity with internal control
(gradually enabling him to be less reactive), and tolerate momentary frustration with limits both from his parents and in exploratory play with his
toys. Henry now had a favorite transitional object: his stuffed toy "Boo
Bear," which he carried everywhere—on airplanes during vacations, car
trips to aunties, overnights with Grannie and Grampie (like Linus'
blanket).

Boo Bear had Henry's scent, along with Mom's, Dad's, and Bozley's
(the dog). When anxious, Henry sucked on Boo Bear's hands and feet, a
comforting taste and texture, Henry's security. He used Boo Bear during
stressful times to help him regain composure. Throughout any given day,
family members saw a wide range of emotions on Henry's face: joy, fear,
curiosity, frustration, anger, pride, surprise, disgust, shame, and exhilara-
tion. He was developing quite a sense of humor. He laughed when Mom
pretended to "gobble up" his tummy; and he imitated her by tickling
others, especially Bozley.

When Henry's mom died, much of his predictable, consistent daily
routine and life rhythm died with her. Despite the genuine love and
concern of his dad, grandparents, and others, Henry had lost his primary
hidden regulators. Without his mother, he spiraled into dysregulation.

Talking to him about Mommy being gone did not help. He did not
understand death. He thought she would return. His emerging language
skills limited his verbal expression as well as his ability to understand
adult responses to *Where is Mommy?*

Henry's thumb-sucking on Boo Bear became frantic. He was no
longer calm. His sleep–wake cycle deteriorated, as did his desire to
explore. Instead, he clung to his dad and grandparents. On his own, he
felt empty and became hyperactive (often a sign of anxiety). He couldn't
pay attention or become absorbed in exploration or play. He couldn't
touch, feel, hear, see, taste, or smell his mommy. He frustrated easily. He
could no longer delay gratification, and he had tantrums more often

which lasted longer. His *No!* became a power struggle for control. Although part of an emerging autonomy, his *No!* protest behavior was also an attempt to regain his mother (Bowlby 1973). *If I don't let you do it, Mommy will return to help me.*

The first three months after her death were unsettling. However, Henry's dad and maternal grandparents sought counseling early on, which helped them identify Henry's hidden regulators (wrapped in his mother's interactions with him) and reweave them into his new world. Doing so allowed his dysregulated physiological distress to return to a more regulated state. With insight into developmental skills, Henry's caregivers were able to design new strategies and structures for him so his life would resume being consistent, predictable, and filled with regulators (routines) upon which he could once again anticipate and depend.

Henry's father's employer allowed a predictable daily schedule, to be available to Henry at the beginning and end of each day: waking, feeding, bathing, and bedtime; all performed at essentially the same time and in the same way to create new and comfortable rituals. Much of the father's excess office work was now completed at home after Henry went to bed.

Henry's maternal and paternal grandmothers took turns coming to his home during the week until he was three and entered preschool in the afternoons. They maintained many of the daily rituals: playtime, eating, and naps, as had Henry's mother.

During all of these interaction times, all the caregivers were now aware of the critical need to stimulate, arouse, and create opportunities to explore his world to support his emerging neuropsychological development. They continued to set developmental limits while helping him develop age-appropriate coping strategies when frustrated, angry, or frightened.

THE DEVELOPING BRAIN

The first two years are indelibly imprinted and "shape the development of a unique personality, its adaptive capacities as well as its vulnerabilities to and resistances against particular forms of future pathologies" (Schore 1994). Remember father of psychobiology D.O. Hebb's "Neurons that fire together, wire together" (1949).

Whatever is repetitive in the first two to three years of life gets hard-wired together. So, loss during these early years must be mindfully addressed, not dismissed with the assumption that the child will not remember. "We live in a sea of sensations that shape our...subjective experience," wrote Daniel Siegel (1999). The early months in life are the time when we create competent and balanced responses to all stressors we will face in society. It is the foundation of affect regulation.

In the first two years of life, the brain grows at almost three times the rate it will ever grow again. Social and emotional deprivation do affect the young brain's development. The first 24 months are critical for healthy maturation (Cozolino 2002; Schore 1994; Siegel 1999; Weaver, Grant, and Meaney 2002). Early trauma, especially without adequate caregiving, can result in later behavioral problems, such as: hyperarousal, aggression (toward self and/or others), reduction in the capacity to cope with disruptions, reduced long-term capacity to modulate physiological arousal, dissociation (numbing, to avoid reliving a trauma), decreased motivation (depression), hyper-alertness to stimuli, hyper-reactions, memory problems; and borderline, narcissistic, schizotypal, or dissociative personality disorders.

From ten months through the second year of life, the orbitofrontal cortex is developing in the brain, a critical area for integrating reason and emotion. Unlike other areas in the brain, the orbitofrontal cortex has less recovery from damage or lack of stimulation during the first two years of life. It is a neurological "Use it, or lose it" window of opportunity (i.e. critical period).

A poorly developed orbitofrontal cortex can result in significant problems in emotional functioning, lack of empathy, inappropriate social behavior, impulsiveness, explosiveness, sexual disinhibition, increased motor activity, difficulty in interpreting facial expressions, self-indulgent attitude (grandiosity); and problems in self-awareness, dissociation, increased risk for addictive behavior, and lack of maternal instinct in childrearing. For the orbitofrontal cortex to grow and develop healthily, a "good enough" caregiver must be available during these critical years.

From age one to two, toddlers are beginning to seek a balance between independence and interdependence. This is an important and dicey challenge when a loss occurs, because it influences later stages, such as peer relations, close friendships, and the ability to have and maintain intimate relationships with significant others. Should separation or a loss occur during this time period, the toddler will experience a sense of abandonment anxiety due to the now developed mental representation of the caregiver (e.g. maternal representation: see Glossary). If unresolved, later losses can trigger this abandonment anxiety.

The primary goal for the first two years is the development of attachment (see Glossary). During the first year, through repetitive interactions with the caregiver, the infant develops the internal expectations of how others will treat her—what Erik Erikson (1963) calls the stage of "Trust vs. Mistrust" (security vs. insecurity). If the parenting is "good enough," the infant learns to trust in the anticipation that the caregiver is available and shows empathetic feelings. Early relationships have the power to soothe or dysregulate, depending upon the quality of the caregiving. The early memories of how we are treated by significant others create indelible memories by which we organize our inner world, both when we are alone and when we are relating with others. Basic research shows that adverse social experience during early critical periods results in permanent alteration in such neurotransmitters (see Glossary) as dopamine, noradrenaline, serotonin, and corticosteroid receptors (Chrouso et al. 2003; Panksepp 1998; Perry 1993; van der Kolk et al. 2006).

"Character armor," named by Wilhelm Reich, founder of somatic psychology in 1945, is shaped during the first years of life and is preverbal (i.e. without language). According to Reich (1945), character armor is our preverbal defenses which are developed during the first years of life. These defenses derive from one's early emotional memories of early experiences, stored in one's sensory, motor, and emotional networks. Such "character armor" can imprison one in rigid and stereotyped reactions as a defense against one's environment. Character armor forms as a result of such things as misattunements, neglect, trauma by significant caregivers, and early losses poorly attuned thereafter. According to Reich, early defenses can shape the levels of our central nervous system, becoming imprinted in our entire body/mind as powerful yet invisible influences.

The foundation of trust ("I'm okay. You're okay.") is acquired around age 9 to 12 months due to the development of a mental representation of the primary caregiver. Only loss after this age leaves the infant feeling abandoned. To feel abandoned, she first must have a mental representation of "other." Before the age of 9 to 12 months, a child feels annihilated when she has lost the primary caregiver's hidden regulators and the attachment experiences with that caregiver. The child experiences life as a jumble of sensations—much like Humpy Dumpty falling off the wall and shattering into a million pieces. There is nothing the child can hold onto to soothe her disrupted sense of the world. The mental representation has yet to be solidly built.

Just because a child may not have an *explicit memory* of an early loss does not mean she has no memory of the significant loss. Indeed, the memories are exquisitely accurate in the *implicit memories* circuits. At a seminar I presented, a man said he always knew something was missing, but his dad and stepmother didn't tell him until he was nine that his mother had died when he was three months old. Until then, he had been told that his stepmom was his biological mom. Despite the lies and poor delivery of the information, the truth had validated the man's implicitly accurate but inexplicable feelings.

There are many kinds of early loss for an infant: the caregiver's death, the biological parents relinquishing the newborn/infant, the caregiver leaving for military service, the mother's post-partum depression, the primary caregiver's grief over a critical loss that caused him or her to be emotionally unavailable to the young child.

A few examples of how infants lose their caregivers without warning are: the collapse of the World Trade Center on September 11, 2001; the Asian Tsunami in 2004; Hurricanes Katrina and Wilma in 2005; the hundreds of civilians killed daily in civil wars, soldiers (mothers and fathers) never returning from duty or returning with post-traumatic stress or traumatic brain injury.

When adults are overwhelmed by the demands of such a loss, everyone suffers. A child suffers now and, if not addressed, the suffering continues into the growing years and into adulthood. Pain is pain. The psyche never forgets. The wound becomes a lifelong burden to manage, weaving in and out of the core sense of self. The psychological wound—like a scar emotionally, in mental processing and decision-making, even in latent health issues—shapes the individual's demeanor, beliefs, and interactions throughout life. It is the fortunate children who have committed caregivers who walk the journey through the "Mickle Woods" with them, supporting them in finding a way to use their inherent traumas to boost personal healing and to surpass their old fears constructively and love again.

In the movie *Star Wars: Episode III—Revenge of the Sith*™, Padme, Anakin's wife, is pregnant. He remembers a dream in which he was told she would die in childbirth. This tosses him violently into a fear of abandonment. He shares his fear with Yoda, who replies that "the fear of loss is a path to the dark side. Anakin should train himself to let go of everything he fears to lose. Yoda's advice is a spiritual detachment, a way to let go of fear. However, Anakin does not accept Yoda's advice, and turns to Palapatine who feeds his fear of abandonment by promising that Padme's death can be avoided if Anakin listens and does what Palapatine commands.

Anakin's own early unresolved loss of his mother is now triggered by the impending loss of his wife, and he regresses to an earlier stage of emotional and moral reasoning. He recites the Jedi code, but is unable genuinely to internalize the rules and soothe his deep fears. Instead, he uses his cognitive reasoning to rationalize his behavior of killing without remorse (an early developmental level, thinking only of his own needs). His primary emotion is fear. His secondary emotion, anger, defends his primitive fear of abandonment…and he becomes addicted to anger within which he feels justified, even powerful. Using threat, intimidation, and attacks to keep his wife alive, he avoids his intense unconscious fear of abandonment. To be healed, he must be willing to face the truth about his early loss and to feel his distress. He must have the courage to hold out through his journey and discover that it will make him stronger, not weaker.

This is the shadow side that all children face who lose their significant caregiver during their first two years. Indeed their fear of future losses can become "a path to the dark side." Like Anakin, if there is no one committed to join them early on in this tragic journey, they too could exhibit behaviors similar to Anakin.

COGNITIVE, EMOTIONAL, AND PHYSICAL CONSIDERATIONS: USEFUL CHECKLISTS

Cognitive reasoning: Sensory-motor reasoning (see Glossary)

Social/emotional reasoning: Trust vs. mistrust

Moral reasoning: Premoral reasoning

General developmental tasks

- Develops the regulation of sleep–wake patterns and hunger cycle.

- Interest in the world, curious about exploring new things.

- Interest in emotions and interactions with others and pets, especially their caregivers' interactions with them.

- Develops sensory-motor systems: vision, hearing, touch, smell, taste, movement.

- Reciprocal interaction, imitation of caregivers' movements, facial expressions, vocal intonations (mirror neurons: see Glossary). They see caregivers/siblings do something, then try to imitate. Enormous amount of new learning occurs as a result.

- Internal mental perception (representation) of caregiver.

- Develops attachment pattern (i.e. attachment personality style).

- Begins to understand uses and meanings of people and things.

- Develops self-regulation—increasing tolerance for stimulation (i.e. arousal levels), adapting to external environment while maintaining internal equilibrium.

- Midway in this phase: Begins to respond to caregivers' gesture and verbal limit setting.

- Toward the end of this phase: An emerging capacity to use words to communicate.

- Toward the end of this phase: Uses words such as "mad" to express anger, gets mad at an "uncooperative" toy.

- Crucial to developing the orbitofrontal cortex, which is experience-dependent upon the caregivers' interactions.

Conceptualizing a loss

- The earliest concept of life and death: All objects are alive.

- Until the infant/toddler has developed object constancy (see Glossary) at approximately 28 months when the hippocampus begins to develop, the form is recognized but recall is only through (implicit) procedural memory (see Glossary).

- From age 0 to 1, the infant is developing the mental representation of the caregiver. Loss during this period results in annihilation anxiety.

- From age 1 to 2, the infant has a mental representation of the caregiver. Loss during this period results in abandonment anxiety.

Understanding a loss

- A loss before nine months may be experienced as annihilation because all of the hidden regulators are gone, which the infant used to maintain a sense of connection and security.

- A loss at one year and beyond is felt as abandonment, because the child has developed an internal mental representation of the primary caregiver.

- Up to approximately 18 to 36 months, form is recognized but memories are implicit only (unconscious, not consciously recalled or recognized but viscerally remembered).

Typical problems from a loss at this age

- Wants to connect with others. Not sure how.

- Decrease in frustration tolerance, impulse control, and attention span.

- Cannot tolerate long periods of intense emotional pain. For self-protection, vacillates between experiencing the loss and engaging in activity.

- Rocking, frantic head-banging, and fast sucking are coping mechanisms to mitigate anxiety and provide comfort. The infant/toddler may have an intense expression, a glazed far-off look. (Normal rocking, head-banging, sucking is calm and rhythmic; facial expressions are joy and contentment.)

- Poor self-regulation. Cannot maintain equilibrium in the face of stimulation, may not seek stimulation, may shut out stimuli. Or may become labile, hyperactive, or unfocused in attempts to maintain contact with the environment.

- Rapid shifts through emotional states.

- Extreme behavioral dysregulation when emotionally aroused.

- Difficulty in developing self-soothing skills.

- Uninhibited behavior (biting, hitting).

- Extreme outbursts.

- Difficulty establishing sleep–wake and hunger cycles.

- Difficulty learning toilet training.

- Poor ability to understand cause and effect.

- Withdrawn, compliant, hyper-aggressive, disorganized.

- Fragmented (Humpty Dumpty effect).

- Polarized (stuck in what to do, how to negotiate all the changes).

- Reduced acquisition of self-awareness.

- Difficulty in re-establishing attachment patterns.

- Disruption in processing senses (can develop sensory processing problems in auditory, visual, tactile, olfactory, kinesthetic, and gustatory domains).

- Delayed language development.

- "All or nothing" reasoning. Result: inflexibility, rigidity in how thinks about things and others. "All good" or "all bad." "All right" or "all wrong."

- Perceives events, situations, and people as partial objects. Identifies with imaginary figures and people who do not regularly participate in her everyday world.

- Prone to form inaccurate impressions of what other people are thinking and feeling and why they act as they do. Misperceives events and forms; mistaken impressions of people and the significance of their actions. Leads to poor judgment in social interactions: fails to anticipate the consequences of her own actions, and misconstrues appropriate behavior.

- Limited ability to identify comfortably and empathetically with real people in her life. Cannot step outside of her own view and needs or to see situations from other perspectives.

- Has worrisome thoughts about being unable to prevent other people and events from determining her own life. Has a disconcerting awareness of needs that are not being met. Recognizes little or no control over her own life.

- Has an impaired ability to concentrate, which later creates adjustment difficulties in learning and work that requires sustained attention.

- Stressful situations are experienced as highly threatening. Stress overload can impair the capacity of self-control and may create impulsiveness in what the child thinks, says, and does.

- Lapses in control usually occur in complex, ambiguous situations where she is uncertain of what is expected; or she perceives a threat of loss of a person, object, or goal. May show rigidity (due to anxiety) when change occurs because she lacks flexibility to adapt to new situations.

- Vacillates between rigid control of emotions and outbursts/tantrums.

- Appears oppositional when stressed; reverts to rigidity and inflexibility.

- Acutely upset, anxious, or disorganized due to undeveloped coping skills.

Considerations to help a grieving infant or toddler

- Identify hidden regulators wrapped in the significant loss. Integrate these hidden regulators into the new caregivers' environments and interactions. Doing so increases familiarity and can reduce the amount of physical, cognitive, and emotional stress caused by all the changes.

- Provide a protective, comfortable, safe environment (i.e. secure base).

- Play simple games that emphasize the senses. This helps the child acclimatize to stimuli, while building a tolerance to increase her arousal levels.

- Through interesting and pleasurable activities, help the child learn to regulate experiences.

- Gaze empathetically at the child and mirror her expressions. Don't be afraid of overempathizing with her grief. Don't try to avoid feeling what she is feeling; avoidance leaves the child more isolated and confused. Supporting the child emotionally is critical.

- If the child has learned self-soothing or self-parenting already, gradually participate while she is comforting herself. This allows you to enter the child's world, and she will begin to associate you with relief. (Example: If head-banging, put a pillow or your hands under the child's head; or gently massage the back of her neck while she is head-banging.)

- Seek a balance between age-appropriate activities and regression. Use play therapy to help resolve fears and conflicts. Teach and support communication.

- Engage rhythmic play, musical songs, repetitive nursery rhymes.

- Stay emotionally involved and available while setting limits on the child.

- Provide lots of pictures of prior caregivers, other children, and the child's home. Children begin to internalize memories at six months. These memories are partial memories, without words, experienced as something "familiar" to them like a "glimpse of something from the past" which as yet to be "parked" in verbal memories. Validate those memories so that they can become "parked" into explicit memories, filling in pieces of the puzzle that were lost (missing).

- Adjust the range and intensity of stimuli to encourage alertness and interest, or to diminish her sense of confusion and feeling overwhelmed. When the child is bored, increase the stimuli. When the child is stressed, decrease the stimuli.

- Avoid prolonged separations whenever possible. Maintain hidden regulators and routines (rituals) during separations. Prepare the child ahead for what will happen. Leave little pleasures, such as tape-recorded messages to be shared at bedtime, cards to look at and be read in the morning, a T-shirt with the caregiver's scent to wear to bed. Call home daily.

- Stabilize sleep patterns (e.g. routine bedtime ritual; swaddle in lightweight, breathable, soft blanket with familiar scent; play tape-recorded repeatable lullabies; bathe with soothing scents). Also, an infant massage (three times a day for 5 to 15 minutes) is calming and releases toxics that build up due to stress (restabilizes the pituitary level). Place a soft misting humidifier in the bedroom, with relaxing scents added to the water (e.g. lavender).

- Create a pleasant eating routine, using healthy, nutritional foods and liquids. Incorporate comfort foods (foods familiar before the loss). There are many hidden regulators in comfort foods: smell, texture, taste, temperature, visual recognition, sound of the food in the mouth.

- Maintain a calm, consistent, and predictable environment and routines in the daily schedule. Provide a "point person" in each setting, who will take responsibility for maintaining (monitoring) the infant in that environment for that time period.

- Monitor that the infant/toddler does not prematurely move into precocious behavior and self-parenting—as a way of not attaching.

- Develop morning waking and evening bedtime routines (rituals).

- Be aware of the child's capacity for arousal. Gradually and gently introduce new or increased sensory stimulations (sight, hearing, touch, smell, taste, movements).

- Assess which senses the child uses to calm herself. Appeal to them to help her become calm, while providing simple stimulations to senses she does not yet seem to be using. Emerging sensory exploration and expansion must be given opportunities and support to develop during these early years.

- If the child shows signs of sensory-processing problems, consider intervention support.

- Create a family story box of her background (objects belonging to the "lost" person (e.g. wristwatch, piece of jewelry, golf club, tennis racket, special cooking utensil; clothing, perfume/cologne they wore often, music they loved; pictures/videos of previous family, positive foster care/orphanage; the journey, days in the new home). Be sure to keep pieces belonging to the child's early years (e.g. lock of hair, special blanket, stuffed toy, rattle, favorite, familiar pieces of clothing). Include feelings and descriptions of activities/events, such as behaviors, smells, sounds, tastes, touch, vision (stored in the unconscious implicit memory). This allows the memories to be discussed once the child is older, which helps her "park" them into the conscious mind (explicit memory) and carry them throughout life.

- If the child is adopted from a different culture or ethnic background, celebrate her heritage (cultural dishes, music, religion, language, books, pictures, toys), blending the child into the new home life.

- If adopted, this is a good time to read books about adoption (animal world, various cultures and countries), along with books like *Love You Forever* by Robert Munsch.

CHAPTER 7

TODDLER THROUGH EARLY CHILDHOOD (AGES 2 TO 6)

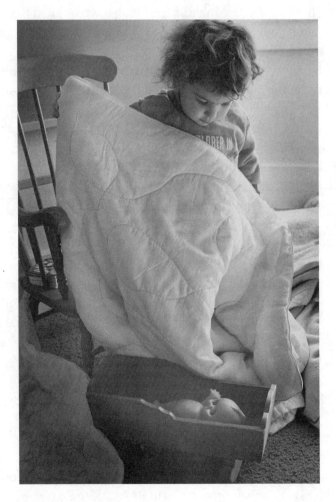

Photo by John Schoenwalter

SARAH'S STORY: MEMORIES OF BEREAVEMENT

At a seminar I taught in Springfield, Missouri in August 2006, Sarah, a woman in the audience, told us of going to live with her aunt and uncle at age three after her mother died. In her adolescent years, she began to have the following recurrent dream.

She dreamed of a young child riding her tricycle up and down the street. She remembered the sensory feeling of pushing the tricycle up a steep incline, and the feeling of the movement of the tricycle moving quickly downward. The child went down the steep incline to an old Victorian home where many people were going inside. She went in, too, and hid behind a wall, peeking into the living room. A lot of folks were in the room but no one saw her. She saw a young woman lying in a casket, wearing a pink dress.

This memory stayed with this woman throughout her life. She didn't remember specific emotions, but she did recall sensing that she knew those folks.

When she was in her late adolescence, she told her aunt about the dream. Upon hearing it, her aunt and uncle took her for a ride to the neighborhood Sarah hadn't lived in since she was three. There was the house she had grown up in until her mother died, situated on a street with a steep incline, similar to the streets one sees in San Francisco. The woman in the pink dress was her mother.

Sarah's aunt and uncle told her the story of the funeral and the house she lived in. As they shared the information with her, a dreamlike recollection that had been "parked" as a nebulous sensation of time and space now became a validated, conscious memory of her deceased mother. A part of Sarah's life puzzle was put in place that day. The partial explicit memory that had floated in her psyche, waiting to be put into its proper place, had arrived home.

SARAH'S EXPERIENCE SHOWS why it is important to create a storybook and story box of the bereaved child's life; it helps place and integrate valued recollections. It helps make sense of the pieces. These boxes and books can include a variety of things: pictures, videos, mementos; and sensory objects, such as a lock of hair, familiar music, comfort foods, favorite blanket, toys, clothes, a watch, necklace, the collar of their pet.

The mementos serve to say, *We existed together… This is not just in my imagi-nation… My belief in being "loved" (i.e. lost loved one) is validated.*

Children aged 2 to 6 do not understand the permanence of death. (*I know Mommy was very sick and doctors couldn't help her, so she died. But when is she coming back?*) Just because a child uses the right words (e.g. *"Mommy is dead"*) does not mean he fully understands the implications. He can tell the story accurately without being able to internalize the idea that *dead* means never to return. The cognitive ability at this age does not allow the child to make that leap of understanding. He also lacks the language to describe what he is feeling and thinking. So, he is unable to ask for what is needed when fearful, angry, empty, lost, and confused. Comfort requires another's comforting presence.

In the past, therapists and caregivers mistakenly interpreted a child's lack of verbalization to mean such things as: "He doesn't remember the loss, the adoption, the changes. No need to bring it up. It will only cause unnecessary suffering for him." (similar to the adage, "Out of sight, out of mind"). However, just because it is out of conscious sight (i.e. explicit memory) does not mean it is out of mind or body (i.e. implicit memory).

Remember, they were there! It happened to them! A lack of verbal-ization does not mean no memory. The memories of the deceased loved ones are usually of visceral sensations, internalized habitual routines and rituals, details but without a coherent whole. They have trouble recalling life and loved ones in a broader context. It feels like déjà vu when the memories rise to the surface; they are familiar, but without specific "parking spaces."

What is your first concrete memory? How old were you? What details do you remember? Details are often hidden regulators and preverbal experiences. Without concrete (explicit) memories, a child can feel cheated, angry, and confused.

Children do not have the capacity to separate, classify, or organize their losses into their larger world. When in distress, they cannot talk about it. They have not acquired the ability to express their deep feelings, thoughts, and emotions in words. Rather, they act out their fear, anger, sadness, emptiness, confusion, and loneliness. Their behavior is immedi-ate and shows in their facial expressions. This is how they work out their grief. They are showing us (i.e. telling us) by their behavior.

This is why it is so important to be *attuned* observers. Your ability to empathize allows you to "walk in their shoes" for a moment, to gain a sense (a feeling) as to how the child is feeling (rather than what he is thinking). This exquisite ability is developed through what neuro-scientists call mirror neurons. Watching a child's facial expressions can offer a window into his heart at the time. As Paul Ekman's research (Ekman 1999; Ekman and Rosenberg 2005) has proven, irrespective of culture, country, or race, facial gestures are universal: anger, disgust, fear, happiness, surprise, sadness.

The early years are critical for a child to become a healthy, adaptable, secure adult (Goleman 1995, 2006). The *Zero to Three Bulletin* of the National Center for Infant Programs reported in 1988 that school success is not predicted by a child's knowledge of facts or ability to read, as much as

> emotional and social measures: being self-assured and interested; knowing what kind of behavior is expected and how to rein in the impulse to misbehave; being able to wait, to follow directions, and to turn to teachers for help; and expressing needs while getting along with other children. (p.45)

Most of the students who do poorly in school, said the report, lack one or more of these elements of emotional and social intelligence, regardless of whether they have a cognitive difficulty or learning disability.

There are seven key ingredients for a child's readiness for school: confidence, curiosity, intention, self-control, relatedness, capacity to communicate, and capacity to cooperate. These ingredients are developed during the first four years and have lasting consequences.

A GOOD FILM for understanding early loss is the French movie *Ponette*, a lovely character study. Ponette is a four-year-old girl who recently lost her mother in a car accident, which she survived. This captivating movie shows the variety of things Ponette does to gain her mother's return. She shifts between engaging with others to withdrawing from others, actively performing magical rites and waiting for proof of their success in her mother's return. She tries magical chants, brings special offerings to her mother's grave, and prays to God to "Tell my mommie to talk to me."

All to no avail. Early one morning, Ponette goes to her mother's grave and digs desperately, crying, "Mama! Mama! I am here."

So often, young children's grief reactions go unrecognized by the adults around them—especially if the adults are struggling with their own grief process. Adults, too, can be overwhelmed by the load they carry after a significant loss.

Little ones at this age often try to comfort rather than burden the adults with their own suffering. They know implicitly that things will remain wobbly until others around them are stabilized. Remember, they too have the exquisite ability to "mirror and gaze" and read the facial gestures of others in their environment. By this age, many of their mirror neurons are nicely developed, because of their early "good enough" caregiving.

We adults must be willing to make the effort to "walk in their shoes." We can move into a child's loss through his eyes, experiences, gestures, and behaviors. In doing so, we will receive visceral feedback (via our body) into how the child may be feeling.

Otherwise, we risk minimizing the child's grief, abstracting his process, or laying over our own thoughts and perceptions as if they are the child's. If perchance we feel we cannot walk the journey emotionally with the child, we owe it to him to offer someone who can and will be supportive during the grief process.

COGNITIVE, EMOTIONAL, AND PHYSICAL CONSIDERATIONS: USEFUL CHECKLISTS

Cognitive reasoning: Preoperational reasoning (see Glossary)

Social/emotional reasoning: (ages 2 to 3) Autonomy vs. shame or doubt; (ages 3 to 6) Initiative vs. guilt

Moral reasoning: Punishment vs. obedience

General developmental tasks

- Does not distinguish fantasy from reality (high imagination and fantasy play).
- Balances between holding on and letting go (toddler).

- Balances between conquering and being overcome (pre-schooler).

- Due to the developed internal mental representations of care-givers, he can use the ability to hold onto the caregivers, who are away for brief periods of time, through these internal memories. The mental representations offer what Mahler, Pine, and Peryman (1975) term as a form of "emotional refueling," access-ing such memories to briefly feel safe and secure, believing he will be reunited shortly.

- Organizes and differentiates imagery about self and others.

- Understands cause-and-effect in sequential, one-direction pat-terns (linear thinking only; cannot do reversible thinking).

- Able to inhibit aggression (short-term).

- Gradually increasing frustration tolerance and impulse controls.

- Aware of colors and shapes, and cause and effect through ac-tion-related responses.

- Aware of present, future, and past (short duration only).

- Draws simple geometrical figures (e.g. square, triangle).

- Draws what he knows, rather than what he sees.

- Gives inanimate objects living attributes.

- Thinks in rigid terms: good/bad, black/white.

- Acts on perceptions without being able to step back and think about it.

- Able to experience two emotions at the same time (e.g. happy/mad, fearful/curious).

- Able to stabilize moods and self-soothe for a short period when mildly or moderately stressed. Gradual emergence of the basic personality.

- Shame develops at ages 2 to 3. Guilt emerges around ages 3 to 4.

- Able to sustain attention (2 to 6 minutes), which increases with maturation. By age 5, can sustain attention for 15 minutes (even for things not highly interested in).

- Able to delay gratification (short periods of time).

- Learns from doing.

- Ages 2 to 3: Seeks to avoid punishment. The physical attributes of an action determine its goodness or badness (e.g. the bigger the damage, the "badder" it is).

- By age 4: Begins to follow rules in games and tell others the rules (should they change or break them).

- Ages 4 to 6: Seeks self-benefit, satisfying one's own needs, occasionally the needs of others. Fairness, reciprocity, and sharing are present but interpreted in a pragmatic way (*"You scratch my back. I'll scratch yours"*).

- By end of this stage, begins developing enduring friendships (which can last a lifetime).

Conceptualizing a loss

- Does not understand the permanence of death (i.e. cessation of bodily functions, such as the person is not breathing, not eating, not moving = dead = never coming home). Still expects Mommy (caregiver) to come home.

- Up to age 3, *all* objects are still alive. At approximately age 3, object constancy develops. Conscious (explicit) memory becomes more available and the child recognizes the emotional ties he has with loved ones. As a result, separation anxiety is experienced as a fear of abandonment and isolation from the loved ones.

- By ages 5 to 6, understanding of life is "anything that moves." Thus, even though a young child tells others, *"My daddy is dead,"* he does not understand the full meaning of the words. Like Ponette told her daddy in the French movie, "There are still holes in the ground from which she can return," magical thinking about the loss still prevails.

Typical problems from a loss at this age

- Because the child cannot pinpoint what is bothering him and what he feels, it often comes out in physical symptoms, such as: excessive activity, complaints of tummy aches, outbursts of anger, feeling of emptiness filled by eating or becoming involved in activities (avoiding other things).

- Additional symptoms of grief:
  - poor understanding of cause and effect
  - high emotionality
  - increased impulsivity
  - poor behavior management
  - increased stubbornness
  - aggression (kicking, hitting, biting)
  - temper tantrums (especially during change or transition)
  - lack of concern for danger or safety
  - dependence on structure provided by adults (reluctance to explore or take initiative, curiosity wanes)
  - rigid thinking
  - extreme difficulty in dealing with change
  - delayed acquisition of preschool concepts
  - minimal-to-no symbolic elaboration
  - shallow and polarized behavior
  - difficulty in reality testing
  - vulnerable mood stabilization
  - fragmented sense of self and others and/or lack of differentiating self from other, or narrow sense of self and others.

- Their coping mechanisms are:
  - regression
  - depression
  - denial
  - displacement
  - fantasy
  - magical thinking (that the deceased loved one will return).

- A child who loses a parent or sibling through death may wrongly believe he caused it. It is essential to monitor the child's experience of shame, so he does not develop toxic shame. Adults must pay particular care to complete the repair phase after setting limits and consequences on the child. The repair phase is returning the child to the feeling that *You and I are OKAY with each other now.* It often involves a brief discussion of what caused the limit or consequence to be enforced, as well as potential solutions (alternative, more appropriate behavior) for the future.

- Often, young children do not have the language to describe their feelings or to ask for what they need. They tend to express through behavior, often regressing to an earlier level of functioning (helplessness) (Moody and Moody 1991).

- They are unable to take much comfort from verbal statements.

- Tendency to become more clingy to others.

- Seeks balance between independence and interdependence, an important challenge at this age. How the grief is addressed influences the child's continued development and in later life peer relations, close friendships, and intimate relationships.

Considerations to help a grieving toddler or preschooler

- Identify hidden regulators wrapped in the significant loss. Integrate the hidden regulators into the new caregivers' environments and interactions. This increases familiarity and can reduce the amount of physical, cognitive, and emotional stress caused by all the changes.

- Be emotionally available to the child's dependence and regression needs.

- Allow the child to keep a memento of the deceased loved one.

- Provide opportunities for the child to participate in memorializing activities.

- Read, encourage, and respond to the child's emotions and behaviors (love, pleasure, assertion; fear, sadness, anger)—while fostering a gradual reality orientation and internalizing limits. (Avoid being overly permissive or punitive.)

- Feelings are personal. Acknowledge the child's feelings. He will then feel accepted and heard, which increases a sense of safety and willingness to communicate. Avoid dismissing the child's feelings, even though the cause–effect reasoning may seem illogical. When dismissing a child's feelings, we run the risk of having him withdraw communication with us regarding the loss. (It is like Saint-Exupéry's *The Little Prince* childhood drawing that failed to be understood by adults. "So I lived all alone, without anyone I could really talk to.")

- Model appropriate ways for the child to express his feelings.

- Answer all questions, both cognitively and emotionally, regarding the child's loss. Try to answer the questions with one sentence responses. Wait to see how each is accepted. Take the child's lead. Don't overwhelm him with too much information at one time, because it is hard to digest. Be concise and concrete in your answers and explanations.

- Create opportunities for balance between fantasy and reality (therapeutic and other settings; home, daycare, nursery school, preschool). Remember, fantasy at this developmental level can be an outlet for creative play and emotional release.

- Use therapeutic play, art therapy, and/or music therapy to explore the child's painful thoughts, feelings, and beliefs (e.g. the

"Pebble Technique" described on pp.99–101 is helpful for exploring sensitive issues; also see Appendices).

- Stabilize the sleep pattern (warm bath before bedtime; consistent, predictable bedtime rituals; calming scents, such as lavender mist in the bedroom; bedtime massage; soft, rhythmic music/lullabies on CD. The Mary Poppins Milk Recipe may help to improve sleep, decrease aggressiveness, and improve mood (see Appendix 3).

- Identify and offer comfort foods, especially during times of distress. Comfort food has many hidden regulators associated with the food.

- Monitor or adjust appetite regulation, especially through the use of offering nutritional foods. May need supplement through a daily child's multi-vitamin (consult physician first).

- Organize the daily schedule in a way that it can be consistent and predictable. This will allow the child to begin to be able to "anticipate" his world again, thereby reducing anxiety.

- Avoid prolonged separations whenever possible. Maintain hidden regulators and routines (rituals) during separations. Prepare the child ahead for what will happen: leave little pleasures, such as tape-recorded messages to be shared at bedtime, cards to look at and be read in the morning, a T-shirt with the caregiver's scent to wear to bed. Call home daily.

- If you use a time-out method of discipline, have the child stay in sight, or at least within talking range, so he won't feel abandoned. (Typical time-out duration is one minute per year of the child's age.) Don't forget to do the repair phase immediately after the time-out procedure.

- If the child shows signs of sensory-processing problems, consider a sensory-processing assessment and intervention support. Occupational therapists and physiotherapists should be able to help, because they are experts in this field.

- If the child is adopted, create a family storybook and story box of his background (e.g. pictures/videos of previous family, positive foster care/orphanage; the journey, days in the new home, clothes, special objects if positive memories of previous placements—toy, pillow, object from friends and foster parents, music, games played). Include feelings and descriptions, such as behaviors, smells, sounds, tastes, touch, vision (stored in the unconscious implicit memory), which allows the memories to be discussed and helps the child "park" them into the conscious mind (explicit memory) and carry them throughout life.

- If the child is adopted from a different culture or ethnic background, celebrate his heritage (cultural dishes, music, religion, language, books, pictures, toys), blending the child into the new home life.

- If adopted, this is a good time to read books about adoption (animal world, various cultures and countries), along with books like *Love You Forever* by Robert Munsch.

CHAPTER 8

MIDDLE CHILDHOOD
(AGES 6 TO 10)

Photo by John Schoenwalter

ANDY'S STORY: LOSS OF A FATHER

When Andy was eight years old, in the third grade, his father died of cancer after struggling 18 months to survive. His dad and mom had talked with him about what was happening, and worked with a hospice-care worker on how to help Andy through the experience. Hospice was a valuable resource both during the dying process and after, helping the family with grieving and resources.

Andy watched his dad go through chemotherapy and radiation, withering away into skin and bones from a robust, healthy, strong man. He tried to be supportive, a "good son," and helpful to his younger sister, Allie.

He appeared to handle the loss of his father in the early months. He returned to school three days after the funeral and had only a mild sleep disturbance. He was thoughtful and helpful to his mother; which is not unusual for children, because they are often quite aware of the additional responsibilities that the surviving parent inherits, as well as the parent's emotional state. (Remember, children are usually quite good at reading other people's emotions due to the mirror neurons. So, when a child asks significant others if they are sad, angry, scared, and indeed one is, it is important to acknowledge it. Denying only closes down communication and trust.)

Andy's family continued to live in the same home. His mother had to extend her part-time job back to full-time. As with many children, Andy did not show significant grief symptoms until after his surviving parent had stabilized. While many of his previous hidden regulators were still available (the scent of his dad's clothes, shaving cream, cologne, familiar foods, objects of his father, family photos, same neighborhood, friends, and school), they were also continual reminders of his father—both comforting and painful memories at the same time.

With his mother having to work longer days, she was less available. So, Andy and Allie spent their after-school hours in an after-school facility until his mom picked them up. As a result, some of Andy's daily routines and rituals changed. Interactions (availability) with his mom, sister, and neighborhood kids were disrupted. The now explicit memories of his father and frequent intrusive memories of events they had shared, and now missed, added to his suffering. Simple yet powerful memories. For example, in the past, Andy's dad had watched him during practice and games; now he wasn't there like Andy's friends' fathers were.

Over time, schedules that changed abruptly, or planned activities that were canceled due to unfortunate circumstances, triggered some meltdowns. Sometimes it was just harder to handle such events than other times.

By the time Andy's birthday arrived six months later, he was exhibiting more emotional signs of losing his father. He was always busy and now threw himself into sports activities with an almost frenzied energy. A natural athlete, sports was one area in which he could still feel confident and competent, so he used it as an outlet to release pent-up stress and tension.

At home, he spent more time watching television and playing video games, and he hurried through his homework without correcting his errors. He missed chores or did them haphazardly; and he teased his younger sister more and played "too hard" during encounters. When Andy's mother enforced consequences to rules he broke, his response was often one of irritation and argumentative comments.

Andy's teachers observed that he was less attentive, he daydreamed a lot, and his work performance was declining. He expressed regret and remorse, his mother and teachers knew he was making an effort to keep himself together, but his posture during constructive criticism revealed tension: chest constricted, holding his breath, shallow breathing, hands fisted, grimaces. His sleep was interrupted by nightmares of monsters and skeletons chasing him or hiding in his closet or under his bed. He would wake just before being grabbed. The hospice worker did periodic check-ins with the family and suggested that Andy have a few sessions with a therapist.

At age nine, Andy had the language and explicit memories to be able to talk about his loss and what life was like now that his dad was gone. In my initial session with him, he brought a picture of his father, which I photocopied so we could do the Puzzle Technique (see pp.144–147) together, to help identify some of the things Andy felt was missing in his life (hidden regulators).

Together, we cut a photo into five pieces. On the backs of the pieces, we wrote (in red ink) activities, routines, and memories of the things he missed the most since his dad's death. One by one, together we put each piece back into place, identifying (in blue ink) who might be able to do these things now with him. This was a sort of Action Plan, identifying missing pieces as well as prospective others who might be willing and able to fill in the pieces with Andy (e.g. activities, routines). After we completed rebuilding the picture, Andy shared the insights with his mother, who helped him tweak the Action Plan, offering suggestions when identified others might not be available.

In further sessions, he and I (along with his mom) tweaked and reworked his new Plan. The Puzzle Technique activity gave him a sense of empowerment at a time when he was feeling fragile and fragmented with his thoughts, feelings, and emotions surrounding the loss of his dad.

I also recommended that Andy be hooked up with a "sports mentor," a sort of life coach, or big brother, who would take an active interest in Andy's sports activities. It was also important that he continue the support offered by the parents of the other boys, who could also drive him to and from events. This provided a regular physical outlet in an arena where he could continue to expand his skills and excel, while maintaining his social interaction with his peers. An after-school tutor met with Andy at his after-school program to help him maintain academic progress so he wouldn't fall behind (or compound a sense of failure in school).

Andy's mother introduced the Mary Poppins Milk Recipe (see Appendix 3) at bedtime, along with a lavender misting humidifier in his room at night to help him sleep. His bedtime routine reintroduced the rituals he had done prior to his father's cancer and subsequent death (a time of less stress).

IN THE MIDDLE-CHILDHOOD STAGE, children learn to negotiate, define, and discriminate themselves from others (Erikson 1963). They compare themselves with their peers; especially based on what they can do, learn, and make. This stage can be very competitive: who is better than and worse than—physically, academically, and socially.

The children define likenesses and differences in concrete ways (e.g. eyes, skin color, size, skill strengths, weaknesses). Before this age, many children insist they are exactly like their parents, even if discrepancies are blatant. For example, a three-year-old adopted Chinese girl will insist she looks like her adopted Caucasian mommy; whereas, a seven-year-old will not.

When differences are noticed, the child may feel inferior and as not belonging, as in the children's fairytale "The Ugly Duckling" by Hans Christian Andersen. This timeless story of a lost and neglected cygnet encourages children who feel like an outsider to find their unique qualities (usually by middle or late adolescence). Feeling like an outsider typically develops during middle childhood, and continues into adolescence when defining one's identity is a developmental goal.

In Jungian psychology, the Ugly Duckling is a type of spiritual root story. It contains a fundamental truth about human development that supports further integration and progress. The Ugly Duckling theme centers on a central figure who suffers from events outside his control—as with a child who endures a significant loss. By middle childhood, core experiences are similar to the Ugly Duckling theme and differences are deeply felt: *"Why am I different from my brothers? Why can't I be like my friends? What must I do to fit in?"*

As the Ugly Duckling's days go by, he becomes more and more unhappy. His so-called brothers don't want to play with him, because he is clumsy. All the farmyard folks simply laugh at him, and he feels sad, lonely—an outcast. Like the Ugly Duckling, children who are adopted, or who had to move in with other relatives, say things like: *"I don't look like anybody in this family. I feel ugly. I don't belong. My parents (or relatives) treat me differently than the other kids in the family. I always have to prove myself. I would be happier if I was with my real mother."*

The adopted child may believe she is "damaged goods," or maybe was kidnapped. As soon as the thought "Something is wrong with me" occurs, it can be quickly followed by this thought: "When you figure it out, you'll abandon me too." During this period, many children don't want to go to summer camp, because they are afraid their parents might leave them there. Thoughts and feelings such as these certainly are not abnormal, but the suffering that ensues, if not shared with a compassionate adult, can fester and create unnecessary stress.

The core self actually develops during the first two years of life. Now, in middle childhood, children cognitively (concretely) are able to recognize how they belong. They compare and differentiate themselves by how they look (i.e. physical appearance), their likes and dislikes, their skills, strengths, and weaknesses. If this sense of belonging is lacking in similarities, they often can feel exiled through no fault of their own, exacerbated by misunderstanding and the cruelty of ignorance and meanness of others.

The loss of a parent is one of a child's greatest fears during the middle-childhood developmental stage, especially if teasing and cruel remarks by peers occur, usually around ages eight and nine. Although children in this stage can be very compassionate, they also can be pretty mean and the peer group affiliation can be quite strong. One minute they are a member of a clique, only to be disenfranchised the next. Social stress begins to heighten at this stage and continues into adolescence. At some point during these years, a child can experience ugly, mean comments from peers pertaining to their loss.

Today, with cell phones and the internet, one's peers can gossip anonymously and viciously, leaving a bereaved child feeling even more vulnerable. Unless she has a strong relationship with a significant care-giver (e.g. relative, neighbor) it is less likely she will tell the adult what is happening. Children at this age do not need someone to "fight their battles," but they do need someone to help them learn how to handle their own battles in a constructive way.

A temporary way we reduce daily stressors is through daydreaming, which is normal at the middle-childhood stage, allowing children to momentarily remove themselves from a situation in which they don't want to be. However, children who have suffered a loss can become lost in the fantasy world and daydreaming can consume their daily activities—as a way to escape and fill up, temporarily calm down, deny intrusive emotional feelings.

Daydreaming bridges layers of denial. Kübler-Ross (1969) identified this stage as "yearning and pining" because of a wandering state of mind and blunted emotions. Daydreaming at the middle-childhood stage is worse for children who experienced a loss at an earlier age—before explicit memories could be consciously formed and retained. Such a child can fantasize very creative stories to fill in the gaps, stories they may incorporate into parts of their autobiographical narrative without any reality testing to verify the fantasies.

Other ways we fill an emptiness are through eating; or becoming consumed in activities such as sports, video games, television, internet, or a combination of multi-tasking which allows us to shift attention continually—diverting focus from anything conflicting or bothersome. We never come to rest on the loss itself.

Today's world is filled with so much stimulation and distraction. Even without a loss, there must be adult supervision to help a child feel safe and to make reasonable decisions among the many choices. If a child's early loss was unresolved, by middle childhood she is at risk of behaving according to, in Jungian's term, "the ugly duckling syndrome." The child goes in search of what is lost, knocking on the wrong doors, even when the experience is negative. She is unable to know which are the right doors, having never developed the internal knowledge. Like the song says, "Looking for love in all the wrong places." In the middle-childhood years, children do not have the maturity to handle intense emotions for long periods of time. Whereas, wholesome adults find outlets that are more acceptable and adaptable.

It is important, therefore, for adults to monitor a child's thinking about her loss, because at this age children blame themselves, which can turn into survivor guilt or toxic shame. The child does not blame who is not there (requires abstract reasoning).

The Pebble Technique, devised by Holly van Gulden and Lisa M. Bartels-Rabb, is a gentle strategy for adults who are helping children with any loss to begin inquiry into what a child is thinking, reading, and encountering with peers. "Pebbles are one-liners, not conversations, that raise an issue and then are allowed to ripple until the child is ready to pick up on it (van Gulden and Bartels-Rabb 1999, p.200). The "pebble line" might be used to identify a behavior, physical attribute, or gifted skill acquired from one's family, ancestors, etc. This is especially relevant for adopted children whose adoptive parents acknowledge and respect their child's biological family and culture.

For example, you see the child drawing a picture and you say *You must have inherited your gift of drawing from your father. He was quite the artist himself.* Such a statement can open the door for the child to talk more about "similarities" and "commonalities" they may have had with the one who is no longer physically present in their lives.

A pebble can be tied to many things: feelings (such as sadness, anger, fear). For example, if you are wondering whether your child is having thoughts (and feelings) about being abandoned because she is "defective," a pebble statement might be *I was reading a book that said it's not unusual for an adopted child to think she was given away by the birth mommy/daddy because something was wrong with him or her.*

Once the pebble statement is given, observe the child for signs that the statement has "struck home." Quietly and calmly watch her body and facial responses. If the pebble "struck a nerve," you will know. If not, the fact that you threw it out allows the child to return to you later (next day, month, even year) to talk more about it. The pebble acts as a springboard for communication between you and the child. It can put words to thoughts and feelings that are too hard for the child to formulate coherently or to share at the time.

I have used the Pebble Technique frequently and successfully in a variety of settings and topics in my work with children and adolescents. On one occasion, I received a call from a mother of a six-year-old girl adopted at birth. Her daughter's hair was falling out. She wasn't sleeping well, nor concentrating at school. Her grades were beginning to fall, and her interest in play had dampened. All of these behaviors were quite out of the ordinary for her. Nothing had changed at home or school.

What had changed was the girl's increased cognitive ability. She could now subtract, which meant, she could look at her adoption through the lens of reversibility. To get to her adopted parents, her birth mother had to "give her up" (i.e. subtraction), not just "give her to" (i.e. addition). So, she was sure she was "defective." What added to her fears was the thoughts of "not knowing in what way she was defective" and her fantasy that her adopted parents didn't know either—but once they did they too would give her up.

Clearly, this is a lot for a six-year-old to absorb, feel, and think about. Despite her expanding cognitive ability, it would have been insufficient to reason through adequately enough to be able to have the courage and sophisticated coping mechanisms to put these thoughts and feelings into words for her parents. Too big a risk! Too much to lose!

We were both on a playground swing set, when I dropped the "defective" pebble statement. Immediately, her swing came to a stop and her chin dropped. The "pebble" was a direct hit. From there, together with her parents, we began the discussion and exploration of the "pebble of defection." We then used a real pebble, one we found on the ground, to begin the exploration. Using a real pebble (i.e. a variation of the Rock Technique, see pp.141–147) allowed us to focus on the issue, without the risk of this six-year-old becoming overwhelmed or fragmented by fear or confusion.

COGNITIVE, EMOTIONAL, AND PHYSICAL CONSIDERATIONS: USEFUL CHECKLISTS

Cognitive reasoning: Concrete reasoning (see Glossary)

Social/emotional reasoning: Industry vs. inferiority

Moral reasoning: Acceptance by others

General developmental tasks

- Peer-group identification—being accepted by others is a central theme: good-boy, nice-girl orientation. Good behavior is what pleases or helps others and gains their approval.

- Competition is "industry vs. inferiority." The child does a lot of comparison during these years: Who is better than whom? Who is best or worst in academics, social, and physical activities?

- Thinks logically and reasons, but has difficulty verbalizing what she is thinking.

- Realizes that actions lead to reactions.

- Realizes that personal experiences are not universal. Understands part and whole relationships, that others may have different experiences and different feelings.

- Emotional focus on effort. Intention has become important.

- Eager to try new things, lots of energy.

- Cognitive functions increase. Can consider several attributes at once, hold one constant while altering another, sort objects in more than one way, consider hierarchal organization. Can think of several qualities at once. Aware that others may have a different point of view. Takes into account motives and circumstances.

- Has definite notions about fairness and propriety. Regards rules as absolute and vitally necessary. Things must be done exactly right or the game isn't fair. Rules are created for everyone to follow.

- Can negate an operation, think of the opposite (reversibility). Thinking is limited to things and ideas that can be altered. Does not include verbal hypothesis or deduction.

- Recognizes the constancy of matter, weight, volume, and number, despite superficial change (conservation).

Conceptualizing a loss

- At ages 6 to 8, children have a better understanding of cause and effect. At this stage, they realize that their loss is permanent and cannot be reversed. Although magical thinking is still part of how they view death, it is used less and less.

- Life equals "things that move by themselves." By age eight, the child is transitioning into the biological properties of what is alive vs. dead.

- Death can be personified as an ugly, powerful monster that can take the child away like it did the loved one (e.g. "boogeyman" in the closet or under the bed).

- Mutilation anxiety (fear of bodily injury, or phobias) can become prominent. Such fears are often intensified, because many children believe bad things will continue to happen to them.

Typical problems from a loss at this age

Behavior symptoms include:

- withdrawal

- increased tantrums and irritability

- aggressive outbursts, followed by deep despair and sadness

- shorter concentration and attention span

- difficulty with transitions

- argumentative

- demanding
- increased impulsivity
- shortened frustration tolerance
- increase in angry feelings and behaviors
- decrease in academic performance
- uneven academic strengths and weaknesses
- poor performance even with extra time and effort on homework
- peer problems (increased altercations or isolation)
- difficulty reading social cues and understanding others' behaviors
- inappropriate social actions and reactions
- acting out during unstructured times
- fear of disapproval in how she grieves
- possible withdrawal from peers, causing increase in social isolation and feelings of loneliness
- increase in tendency to become mentally inflexible, and/or disorganized
- feeling of helplessness
- difficulty in pinpointing what is bothering her and what she is feeling
- tendency to identify with the deceased.
- Girls tend to be jealous, stubborn, sullen, irritable, and easily embarrassed.
- Boys tend to be disobedient and show off or clown.

Physical symptoms include:

- excessive activity
- complaints of stomach aches
- feeling of emptiness with attempts to fill the gap with emotional eating; consumed by activity (sports, television, video games, etc.)

- difficulty sleeping/nightmares

- poor appetite, hypochondria

- hair falling out.

Loss of a parent is one of the greatest fears in childhood. If one parent is "lost," the child is at risk of either clinging to the surviving parent or trying to separate in a precocious manner in attempts not to feel so vulnerable. In the former, a child could be misidentified as "school phobic," when in reality it is separation anxiety due to a fear that if she leaves the surviving parent, something bad will happen to that parent, too.

Children can sometimes also over-identify with the deceased and regress to an "all good" or "all bad" evaluation of the deceased in similarities and comparisons. This is one way a bereaved child keeps the person alive in her memory. A child will also look back at the past to gain a sense of personal connection to family and humanity—a natural search for identity.

A child's implicit and/or explicit memories of painful moves or abuse can cause her to be very angry during these years. Anger functions as a defense against feeling the pain of the loss and against the vulnerability to any future separations and losses. She may not allow herself to become too close to another again. Until this problem is identified, acknowledged, and addressed, the anger can keep her from healing and can hinder future attachments.

The middle-childhood child manages separation anxiety by using high levels of fantasy and denial. Although daydreaming is a common pastime in elementary years, for a child in grief it can become a vehicle of yearning and pining for the could-have-beens, would-have-beens if the loss hadn't occurred. There is also the daydreaming that she still might be reunited with the lost loved one. If the loss was at a preverbal time (ages 0 to 2), there are no explicit memories, making it easier to create stories to fill the gap.

Adopted children

- A child who is the "chosen one" believes someone first chose not to keep her. This occurs around ages 5 to 6 in girls, 6 to 7 in boys. They ask *Why?* and *Whose fault?* If the child blames herself, toxic shame can develop. This is also true when a biological child believes she caused a parent or sibling's death (she cannot blame who is not here). Feelings of rejection, toxic shame, not being "good enough," or the need to be "perfect" hinder emotional and social development.

- Children with no memory of their birth parents rarely grieve for the birth father until they work through sadness and anger about the birth mother.

- Due to the need to learn "stranger danger" (e.g. preschool concept of the "boogeyman"), adopted children sometimes combine what they know about their adoption with what they know about kidnapping…and conclude that they were kidnapped.

- Internationally adopted children can feel a great degree of difference between themselves and their new peers and families. Logical reasoning observes a variety of things about themselves that no one else in the family or peer groups shares (e.g. eyes, skin color, size, stature).

- International and ethnically different children identify how they are different physically. They wonder if they were not attractive enough for their birth parents to keep. When raised in a predominantly white community, they sometimes become confused about their racial or ethnic identity. All of this is harder with a child who has special needs. Prior to age six, many of these children believe they are white. Peers (especially ages six and seven) use race as ammunition in interpersonal conflicts.

Considerations to help a grieving child

- Allow the child to keep a belonging of the loved one.

- Provide memorializing activities in which the child is involved in the planning and implementation. Letters, photos, videos, tapes of the past are helpful.

- Read books together about loss and separation to help the child recognize her feelings, which will help during later stages to process the earlier loss. For example, *Did My First Mother Love Me?* by

Kathryn Ann Miller (ages 4 to 8), *The Mulberry Bird* by Anne Braff Brodzinsky (ages 4 to 12), *It's Time to Let You Know* by Beth Riedler (ages 6 and up), *Double-Dip Feelings* by Barbara S. Cain and Anne Patterson (end of preschool years to 10). Movies with similar content are also great ways to help in this journey. Storytelling and movies allow a child to place herself within the story, while minimizing the need for elaborate defenses.

- Children ages 6 to 10 need to understand who has the power. If she believes she could have prevented the death or loss ask, "How do you think you caused this?" Listen attentively, then gently challenge the magical thinking; help the child clarify her previous limitations and abilities (e.g. examples of what a baby, toddler, or preschooler could do in a similar situation).

- Anger is often expressed through behaviors that are not socially acceptable and can be frightening (e.g. hitting, kicking, stomping, yelling, throwing objects). Dealing with the child's anger is essential (and hard to handle at times). Recognize that feelings at this age often require a physical outlet, because they do not have the neurological maturity to handle intense emotions. Teach the child acceptable ways to express anger. Encourage verbalizing emotions, and help the child find acceptable physical outlets. For example, throw foam blocks, punch bags, scream into a pillow, tear up old magazines, scribble vigorously on paper, jump on a mini trampoline, vigorously exercise (instills a lifelong outlet). In addition, help the child learn how to take her own momentary "time out" in order to calm down sufficiently to be able to address the anger in a calmer manner. In calmness, she has a greater access to higher cognitive thinking to deal with the more difficult emotions. Time outs can include: deep breathing techniques supported by concrete props, such as calming aromas or stress balls, short walking meditations techniques, Tai Chi moves using focused awareness of breath and body.

- Set limits on anger expressions that involved aggression, self-harm, harm to others or pets, destruction of property. Place appropriate behavior boundaries. Limit-setting can start with the phrase: "The rule is…" This is the stage of *fairness* in which rules are perceived as absolute and necessary. Validate the child's feelings, while also letting her know that not all expressions of anger are acceptable. Praise the child whenever she expresses anger appropriately. If a limit is set, it must be followed through. And remember, after the consequence, the adult must complete the limit setting by repairing the relationship (i.e. talking about the incident in the hope of understanding the triggers, and helping the child find more appropriate alternatives to expressing anger). It is essential for the child to know "you love her," you just don't love that particular behavior.

- If the child is filling emptiness with overeating or excessive activity, discuss how this is a common reaction to avoid unpleasant feelings at her age. Let the child know that these feelings may return. Help her identify other ways to fill the emptiness (e.g. talk about the feelings, cry, hug, cuddle with her teddy bear, stuffed animals, or pet). Teach that these are coping skills that will re-instill good feelings and safety. *Note:* Consider using the Pebble Technique (see pp.99–101) to broach the subject of overeating or excessive activity. For example: *I've read that kids who have suffered great losses often try to fill their feelings of emptiness by (wanting to eat a lot) or (needing to be doing tons of activities).*

- Monitor nutrition, exercise levels, and social participation. In monitoring the appetite, incorporate comfort foods (from the earlier safe time in life) into the daily nutrients. Remember, comfort foods are rich with hidden regulators (i.e. smell, taste, texture, temperature) wrapped in pleasant memories. If appetite deteriorates, consider using vitamin supplements (by consulting with the child's family physician). In monitoring activities, incorporate recreational hobbies and group play. Physical activity in appropriate balance releases toxins and strengthens health and the immune system.

- Identify and incorporate past hidden regulators in current environmental settings (i.e. rituals, routines).

- Respond quickly to signs of depression. (If necessary, be prepared to solicit outside support through the family physician or a referral to a child therapist.)

- Stabilize the sleep cycle as soon as possible. Do not let sleep problems go on too long (two or more weeks), because it can evolve into a full blown sleep disorder. Explore night-time rituals that may help her body calm down (e.g. warm bath, Mary Poppins Milk Recipe, small water fountain mister in bedroom with calming scents, gentle massage, calming background music in room). Avoid any form of caffeine and sugar three hours prior to bed. Because each child is different, it takes a trial-and-error exploration period to see what combination of strategies work best.

- If the child is spending excessive time daydreaming, inquire into what she is daydreaming about. This may add insights into the child's shattered dreams, yearning for missing hidden regulators, magical thinking surrounding the loss, what she would have done differently, thoughts about how she could miraculously recover the lost loved one.

- For toxic shame and survivor guilt, help the child identify someone who had a similar experience. Allow her to spend time with that person in exploring how she is handling the loss.

- For adopted children, the *W.I.S.E. Up Powerbook* by Marilyn Schoettle is helpful in discussing life changes.

- Bring out the child's storybook and story box (objects, pictures, videos, facts about the personal and genetic history, adoption papers). Allow the child to have her storybook readily accessible, as well as an object belonging to the deceased. It is best to keep the original copy of the storybook and valuable memorable items in a safe place until she is older. Sometimes, when angry or confused, a child will tear up parts of the storybook or destroy the story box in an impulsive moment, only to experience deep regret once the emotion has passed.

- Adopted children need to hear that their birth parents have feelings, too. Talk about how they may have felt (or did). This gives the child permission to have feelings about the life change.

- If the adopted child has not already asked about the past by age eight or nine, using the Pebble Technique (see pp.99–101) will help to identify possible concerns she may have thought or felt but was too vulnerable to state or ask. This becomes a gentle way to help her discuss what was emotionally buried.

- Remember the adage, "What one resists, persists." If the facts of the deceased loved one's past have to do with ancestral stories the child may be at risk of inheriting (e.g. substance abuse, learning disability, genetic predisposition to physical or mental illness), it is better to begin to share (sparingly) some facts so she can be prepared to handle the risk in a more wholesome way should it emerge during adolescence.

- With an adopted child, consider a "search" to gather information about the birth parents. This is not returning the child to the birth parents. In middle childhood (i.e. elementary years), this search poses fewer problems than later during adolescence, because it allows the child time to process what she learns, while still strongly focused on the new family.

- With an international or ethnically different adopted child, help her identify how to accept differences from the new family or culture; for example, with books such as *Chinese Eyes* by Marjorie A. Waybill, *Why Am I Different?* by Norma Simon or *We're Different, We're the Same* by Bobbi Jane Kates. Also offer opportunities to participate in cultural events and historical classes.

CHAPTER 9

ADOLESCENCE TO YOUNG ADULTHOOD (AGES 11 TO MID-TWENTIES): AN OVERVIEW

Adolescence represents an inner emotional upheaval, a struggle between th e eternal human wish to cling to the past and the equally pwerful wish to get on with the future. — Louise Kaplan

THE AGE OF TRANSITION

Adolescence is a transitional stage of human development, the period in which the child matures into an adult. This transition involves biological (i.e. puberty), cognitive, social-emotional, and moral consciousness changes. Adolescents experiencing loss at this stage can feel even more intensely the push and pull of this "holding on and letting go" transitional stage. As Dickens wrote, "Life is made of ever so many partings welded together."

Grieving adolescents face five core issues for developing coping mechanisms, which vary according to their maturity (Fleming and Adolph 1986):

1. Trust in the predictability of events, graced by their expanding abstract reasoning.

2. Gain in a sense of mastery and control, a sense of being in control of their destiny.

3. Forging of new relationships, marked by belonging to a social group, a career/vocational community, an intimate partner, and/or spiritual affiliation.

4. Development of a confident self-image, what Daniel Siegel (1999) terms "complexity"—the ability to be flexible, tolerant of diversity, capable of reflecting on the wholesome and unwholesome aspects of oneself in a responsible manner.

5. Belief in the world as fair and just. In today's international, interdependent, accessible world, this becomes even more complicated yet necessary to develop.

Adolescents regard themselves as the center of the universe—"yet at no time in later life are they as capable of so much self-sacrifice and devotion;" they form passionate relationships and throw themselves enthusiastically into life, yet they have an overpowering "longing for solitude;" they vacillate from "blind submission to some self-chosen leader and defiant rebellion against any and every authority" (Freud 1948). They are material-minded, at the same time idealistic; ascetic but indulgent; rough and inconsiderate but extremely touchy. Moods veer from optimism to pessimism and apathy.

Expansion of the frontal lobe of the brain in adolescents develops hormonal growth from child to young adult in all ways: socially, spiritually, cognitively, and physically. The way an adolescent handles this period is highly personal. Changes may be gradual, or sudden and dramatic. The emerging adult experiences life in greater depth, with expanding ways of perceiving, analyzing, conceptualizing, and hypothesizing.

Again in love with the world, as when age two and three, this time he believes he can do anything, solve any problem (given the opportunity)…and if it isn't given, he will create it.

At the same time, coupled with a sense of "omnipotentiality" (Pumpian-Mindlin 1970) is a feeling of fragility. Pimples on the face make him embarrassed to go out and face the world. Hormonal changes make teens irritable, morose, harshly critical, judgmental, and agitated. Peer relations fluctuate with intense mood swings, while negotiating the experiences of dating, coupling, and sexual urges. Added to all of this is the multi-tasking stimulation of a computer world—the internet, cell phones, iPods, all vying for attention.

Too much stimulation can actually decrease the ability to focus and practice intimate conversations with peers and adults. Multi-tasking can become "multi-dividing." The youth then appears scattered and unable to solve problems, especially when concentrated focus is required.

Peer groups and special friendships (which can last into the adult years) are as important as family. Losses tend to increase during the adolescent years. By the time adolescents today finish high school, most of them have experienced the loss of a classmate: some by car accident, some by suicide, some by alcohol/drug overdose, some by violence. Various high-profile incidents since 1999 (e.g. Columbine High School killings, 9/11 World Trade Center, war in Iraq, Hurricanes Katrina and Rita, the Asian Tsunami, and Virginia Tech massacre) have increased the feeling of the fragility of life and the magnitude of threat and danger. Their world is no longer as safe as they once perceived it. They are exposed—via television, internet, travel—to more possibilities…and more tragedy.

It is essential to recognize the number of deaths today's adolescent can experience, the quality of those relationships, and the time span of those deaths. Death is an irreversible loss. The adolescent knows this. There is no more magical thinking.

In the United States, adolescents spend more time with peers than with family. Adults must be aware of resources for times of crisis (both wholesome and unwholesome resources).

COGNITIVE, EMOTIONAL, AND PHYSICAL CONSIDERATIONS: USEFUL CHECKLISTS

Cognitive reasoning: Abstract reasoning (see Glossary)

Social/emotional reasoning: Identify vs. role confusion

Moral reasoning: Maintain the social order

General developmental tasks

- New defense mechanisms:

    ○ *asceticism*—using spiritual ideals and goals as a coping skill. Asceticism is related to standards of beauty and art. Quality is more important than quantity; one can place stringent prohibitions and standards on one's desires

- *intellectualization*—a mental mechanism in which the youth ·engages in excessive abstract thinking to avoid confrontation with conflicts or disturbing feelings (e.g. uses books, while fulfilling a narcissistic desire to be bright)

- *reaction formation*—adopting affects, ideas, and behaviors that are opposite of impulses harbored either consciously or unconsciously. For example, excessive moral zeal may be a reaction to strong but repressed asocial impulses.

- Reasons abstractly. The ability to think about and cognitively manipulate events, things, or concepts that are not in one's immediate presence or environment.

- Considers many aspects of a problem simultaneously.

- Able to plan and carry out complex projects.

- Able to analyze, hypothesize, and synthesize information symbolically.

- Learns new information independently.

- Develops individual identity.

- Increased autonomy and responsibility for self and others.

- Relative moral reasoning. Begins to view rules as more complicated. May change rules if the group believes it is in the best interest of the group.

- Views punishment as relative, based on intent or the provocation.

- Sees right behavior as doing one's duty, showing respect for authority, maintaining the social order for its own sake (including the wider community by mid to late adolescence).

- Brain development during adolescent years:

  - The adolescent brain is changing. Although by age six, the brain is 95 percent of its adult size, the gray matter, or thinking part of the brain, continues to thicken through childhood, similar to a tree growing extra branches and roots. It is this process of gray matter growth that peaks around age 11 in girls and age 12 in boys. This is about the time of puberty.

Following this peak, the brain begins to prune the excess connections in this gray matter. It is a sort of "Use It or Lose It" principle. Remember Hebb's axiom (1949): "Neurons that wire together, fire together." That means that whatever activities an adolescent indulges in are the connections that will be hard-wired into the brain. So the art of being a "couch potato," a musician, an athlete, a computer geek, etc. will be nurtured.

○ Just at the time that the brain is most vulnerable due to all this new growth and pruning, it is also the time when adolescents perceive themselves as "invulnerable" and tend to try high-risk activities (including high-risk sports activities, alcohol, drugs, speeding in cars). Thus, as Jay Giedd, a neuroscientist at the National Institute of Mental Health, suggests, such high risks may not just be affecting their brains for that day; they may affect the next 80 years (Gogtay et al. 2004)!

○ The cerebellum, that part in the back of the brain, long considered to be involved in the coordination of muscles and physical activity, now is believed to be involved in the coordination of the thinking process. Research is indicating that this area undergoes significant growth and change during the adolescent years. As such, it may be important to get up off that couch, away from that computer, and *move* physically.

Conceptualizing a loss

- Ages 11 to 12, young adolescent transitions from "biological properties" of what is living and dead to abstract reasoning of "what is being vs. nonbeing."

- Early and middle adolescents (ages 11 to 17) often have deficits in risk perception and risk-taking. Although they understand the finality of death, they tend to think it does not apply to them, their family or friends. Over time, experience increases their awareness and expands more mature coping skills.

- By middle to late adolescence (ages 15 to mid-twenties), more scientific information is incorporated into their conceptualization of loss. This can help to lessen anxiety.

- Abstract reasoning can also heighten anxiety due to the youth's increased awareness of death's finality and death's universality. Adolescents can think about death in an increasingly abstract, conceptual, and formal way.

Typical problems from a loss as an adolescent

- The type of loss must be evaluated (e.g. parent, sibling, close friend, school/clubs/sports friendships) which define his adolescent identity. It is no longer atypical that one will experience several losses before this stage is completed.

- Survivor guilt.

- Loss at this stage has close similarities to the challenges and developmental tasks faced in adolescence. Sugar (1968) described adolescent loss as involving the process of protest, searching, disorganization, and reorganization. The adolescent now has double jeopardy in confronting and coping during this stage.

- If the adolescent had experienced significant losses in the past, impending separation from his family can increase the sense of separation anxiety and abandonment, which can disrupt the emerging challenges of identity processes. Old losses can become resurrected with new losses, because it is the reworking of prior losses now at the abstract reasoning level. The new loss serves as the triggering force to again process earlier separations, deaths, etc. Spending time grieving can distort other developmental tasks.

- Uneven cognitive skills and learning deficits, because grief takes time and often changes routines.

- The adolescent is at risk of returning to increased dependence on others, or pushes to emancipate early.

- May cause a reduced ability to assume responsibility, or increased need to take on major parental roles of which he is cognitively and emotionally unprepared.

- Increased anxiety and fears over time compared to peers who have not sustained a loss.

- Social isolation from his peers. If this continues too long, a sense of loneliness (physically and psychologically) will ensue.

- Reduced spontaneity.

- Increased difficulty with managing frustrations of typical adolescence coupled with grief process.

- Due to the physiological changes occurring in the adolescent body, loss at this time can influence the immune system, making the youth more susceptible to illness, and increasing recovery time.

- May attempt to fill the emptiness, assuage the guilt, dampen the anger, diminish the pain of depression, through increased sexual activity, alcohol/drugs, and/or dangerous risk-taking behavior.

General considerations to help a grieving adolescent

- Provide opportunities to participate in memorializing activities, as well as activities that can "make the world a better place" in memory of the deceased.

- If there are "ancestral stories" surrounding the deceased, which the adolescent is manifesting (or at high possibility of manifesting), wholesome or unwholesome, discuss them honestly and openly. This can allow the adolescent to make a conscious choice to continue or change the story. (For example, strengths and weaknesses of the deceased, genetic medical concerns, genetic mental health concerns.)

- Help the youth meet with peers who have experienced a similar loss.

- Support the youth in learning how to respond to people who ig-nore his grief, or who tell him to "get on with life," or tell him that it isn't good to continue grieving.

- Use books, videos, art, poetry, journal writing, photography, music, etc. as outlets to support the adolescent in dealing with his grief.

- Remember that this is a highly stressful period, with changes in: cognitive/academic demands, hormones, and emotional and so-cial demands. Increased stress due to a death can compromise the youth's health and immune system. It is important to monitor his susceptibility to illness, and to seek appropriate medical support in a timely manner.

- Monitor nutritional, exercise levels, and social participation (e.g. vitamin supplements).

- Stabilize sleep–wake cycle. (Yes, even though you know he is now more diurnal (active during the day, sleeps at night) this cy-cle still needs to be evaluated and addressed.)

- Monitor possible substance abuse. Seek referral support as needed (e.g. physician, substance-abuse counselor).

- Guard against internet chat rooms where the youth can contact adults who would use his vulnerability and lack of experience and place him in danger.

- Become familiar with the typical activities that adolescents are using as diversions, social gatherings, and peer-pressure explora-tions. These can be potentially quite dangerous and destructive during this period, especially if he is trying to avoid emptiness, anger, anxiety, depression, or fulfill a need to belong to a peer group during the grief process.

- Allow him to select and keep a belonging of the deceased loved one. At this developmental stage, the belonging should have multiple symbolizations that represent personality characteristics linked to implicit and explicit memories.

CHAPTER 10

EARLY ADOLESCENCE
(AGES 11 TO 15)

Photo by Nhat Meyer

KELLY'S STORY: DEATH OF A BROTHER

Frankie was Kelly's guardian angel. He watched out for her as a baby, held her when their dog, Oscar, died, stood up for her when she was hassled…and teased her relentlessly. Frankie was Kelly's hero and she was his "little sister," no matter how tall she was now.

After the collapse of the World Trade Center in New York City on September 11, 2001, Frankie enlisted in the military. He wanted to help his country. He wanted to keep Kelly safe. Two weeks before his tour of duty ended, three days before Kelly's 13th birthday, Frankie was killed by a roadside bomb. The violent death devastated Kelly and her family, and nightmares haunted her sleep.

News of the war continually reminded Kelly of her brother. As the weeks went on, she was afraid of forgetting Frankie's face and memories of their times together. How could she honor him if she forgot what he looked like? It felt like betrayal.

Kelly's friends were a tremendous support; but after a few months, they resumed their normal lives and wished she would, too. Kelly felt less a part of the group. Intense sadness, anger, helplessness, hopelessness, vulnerability, fear, and despair weighted her every day and night. Her mourning was just beginning.

COGNITIVE, EMOTIONAL, AND PHYSICAL CONSIDERATIONS: USEFUL CHECKLISTS

General developmental tasks

- First attempts at establishing a more distinct identity and separating emotionally from the family. Turns more toward peers for a sense of belonging, usually processed through negative comparisons regarding family (e.g. "I'm not like ___."). Remember how easily embarrassed they are by family members with their friends!

- Can be a period of overwhelming self-doubt. Feels like the ending of the cocoon phase and the emerging of the butterfly—can be quite confusing, unfamiliar, and uncomfortable in their own body and mind.

- Conflict between what they desire (independence) and fear (giving up dependency).

- Worries about what will happen, how they look physically, what their friends are doing, etc. Worries feel monumental, partially enhanced by hormonal changes.

- Role experimentation. Practices being different from the family…and being away from the family; dress, mannerisms, speech, hairstyle, and music become mediums of exerting independence.

- Abstract reasoning is at an extreme level. One has yet to gain sufficient experience to know that the majority of what she worries about will not happen.

- When presented with the facts, she can state how her past and present behavior has had and will have an effect on the present and future outcome. The details are more concrete at this early adolescent age than abstract.

- With minimal support, she can begin to consider several concrete and abstract choices, narrowing the options to two choices, and then make a final choice (deductive reasoning).

- Using resources (textbooks, workbooks, library, internet), the individual begins to become more independent in comprehending, applying, and analyzing both concrete and abstract information.

- Without having to be confronted with wrongdoings, the individual accepts responsibility for her behavior and realizes that her actions may have an impact on future situations.

- The individual pulls from many sources to create a new interpretation of beliefs.

Typical problems from a loss as an early adolescent

- *Eleven-year-olds* are moody, easily embarrassed, see parents as highly flawed and a liability to be hidden from peers. Thus, they may tend to use peers as major support. If they are uncomfortable discussing the loss with their family, their reality testing may be flawed.

- *Ages 11 to 12* are transitioning from how to imagine living beings (biological) to the abstract nonbeing. It is not hard to regress back momentarily to earlier conceptualizations of loss in the hope of salvaging parts of their shattered dreams.

- *Early-to-middle adolescents* have a deficiency in risk perception, which is counteracted only by broadened experience and increased coping skills, such as intellectualization and asceticism. If a loss is overwhelming a youth's emerging sense of self, she may take impulsive risks in trying some questionable adolescent diversions. Hormonal changes, coupled with intense grief processes, can magnify her emotional and physical states. As the adolescent's experiential foundation is poorly lacking, so is judgment, resulting in her taking even higher risks than ordinary prior to the loss.

- A common time when grief over lost birth parents resurfaces. If adopted, increased searching and yearning can emerge again. This can be part of the process of "identity" and "role" confusion.

- A previous death can create a great anxiety for an adolescent preparing to begin emotionally separating from the family (beginning as young as 13).

- Returns to rigid, inflexible thinking.

- Lost or reduced spontaneity.

- Difficulty managing frustrations and disappointments.

- Uncertainty about who she is *now*.

- Returns to increased dependence on others, or pushes to emancipate early.

- Reduced ability to assume responsibility, or takes on parental roles.

- Survivor guilt.

- More anxious and fearful than peers.

- Isolates self from peers, lonely.

Considerations to help a grieving early adolescent

- Increase structure in the environment. May need to return to a prior stage for structure, because it is more familiar and, thus, can be comforting because the youth may wrap around more hidden regulators.

- Limit homework. This may mean same tasks but less of it (e.g. instead of three pages of math, it might be one page of practice). Prioritizing the essential homework to maintain academic development may be required at times.

- Provide opportunities to talk with nonfamily members about the emotional impact of the loss. These opportunities can incorporate others who have had similar losses.

- Teach how to respond to people who ignore the grief or say to the youth "Get on with your life" or "It isn't good to continue grieving."

- Be alert for signs of depression. Proactively intervene.

- Be alert for signs of isolation. Offer opportunity for leisure skill development in a variety of areas (e.g. music, sports, art).

- Identify clear, predictable, and consistent roles and responsibilities for school and home. This can help the youth maintain boundaries in which she can journey through the grief process.

- Assess her needs based on the type of loss: parent, sibling, close friend, or peripheral friend. What was the content of the shattered dreams?

- Offer fiction and nonfiction books (or movies) that describe many kinds of loss, such as *Bridge to Terabithia* by Katherine Paterson, *Say Goodnight, Gracie* by Julie Reece Deaver, *Shira: A Legacy of Courage* by Sharon Grollman, *The Sunday Doll* by Mary Francis Shura, *Tiger Eyes* by Judy Blume.

- Help or encourage keeping a journal, writing a letter, creating a collage, composing a poem, building a scrapbook, acting theatrically, composing a song.

CHAPTER 11

MIDDLE ADOLESCENCE
(AGES 15 TO 17)

Photo by John Schoenwalter

HANNAH'S STORY: DEATH OF A PARENT

At 16, Hannah was moving through her adolescent journey of "Who am I?" when her mother died. This was supposed to be a time when she would begin to move away from the family system, create her own identity, explore new roles, think of college and her future career.

She was the oldest of three siblings: her brother, Taylor, 12; and a younger sister, Mattie, 9. With her mother gone, Hannah took on additional responsibilities for her siblings: doing the majority of the laundry, grocery shopping, and cooking. This was all on top of her school work and a part-time job.

The daily demands became overwhelming and exhausting, and shortened Hannah's time to "refuel" with friends, focus on the academic demands of her honors courses, and earn extra money she was putting away for college...now a lost anticipation.

She had once been "on top of her game." The game had changed—without notice, without directions, and without anyone she believed she could turn to, to share the "multiple losses" caused by her mother's death...and not feel guilty in doing so. Hannah's sense of competence, confidence, and optimism gradually decreased. A sense of emptiness and isolation increased. The loss of her mother reverberated throughout her life.

In such an overloaded state, how could she grieve her mother? Her dad was kind and considerate, but he was overwhelmed, too. The household had been financed by both spouses, and duties shared by both. Now he was the sole provider and caregiver, with their extended family spread throughout the United States and no one nearby to help.

Hannah's teachers shared their concerns with her father about her dropping grades, suggesting it might be due to depression and that a therapist might help. That's when I began to work with Hannah.

She was depressed—overloaded and overwhelmed. In the first sessions, we focused not on the grief process for her mother, but on identifying the varied tasks her mother had performed to maintain the family, which had disintegrated and which Hannah was trying to hold together.

Some of our initial sessions included Hannah's father and the younger children, because they also had been shaken and disrupted by the mother's death. Honoring the family unit's ability to share in the problem-solving also helped to stabilize Hannah. Through creative problem-solving techniques for family members and identifying supportive resources, the gaps were being addressed and Hannah was able to relinquish some of the additional demands.

Using the Puzzle Technique (see pp.138–141), we discovered the missing pieces (hidden regulators) caused by Hannah losing her primary life model and guide, and the ramifications of the additional load each family member was carrying. We problem-solved alternative resources to help her fill the tasks and still focus on her emerging adolescent needs, to keep her on schedule with her developmental growth. Her academic coursework improved, several of her peer-group activities resumed, and the dream of attending college out of state became realizable.

By focusing our initial sessions on the hidden regulators (wrapped in routines) that Hannah and her family had lost by the mother's death, she and they were all able to identify their personal shattered dreams and begin the process of making sure some of those dreams were reinstated. So, their feelings of competency and capability rose to even higher levels. They were traveling through a significant loss, and surviving in a wholesome, loving fashion.

With the family stabilized and reintegrated with common values, Hannah could now allow herself to emotionally mourn the loss of her mother—her guiding light—and begin to realize her own guiding light from within—found in cooperative healing, sharing, and support.

COGNITIVE, EMOTIONAL, AND PHYSICAL CONSIDERATIONS: USEFUL CHECKLISTS

General developmental tasks

- Begins the practice of intimacy through platonic and romantic friendships.

- Forgoes identity set by parents, compromises society's demands.

- Identity vs. role confusion. Questions morals and ideas and future goals, to consolidate sense of self.

- Approach/avoidance behavior in relationships as experiences of closeness, especially with the opposite sex or romantic partner, create a sense of elation and vulnerability.

- Hormonal changes and emotional/cognitive struggles can heighten depression created by the teeter-totter rhythm of this stage.

- Academic accomplishments become more consolidated as the youth is gaining increased awareness of his own strengths, weaknesses, interests, and dislikes.

- Awareness of evolving as a self emerges as he attempts to consolidate his own story, woven from past experiences, present situations, and future possibilities.

Typical problems from a loss as a middle adolescent

- Judgment and reasoning difficulties.

- Does not feel safe to separate from the family physically or emotionally.

- Uneven cognitive skills and learning gaps may occur due to the demands of the grief process. At the time, however, the results can include: lower grade-point average for college admissions and scholarships, decreased scores on entrance exams, difficulty sustaining increased academic demands. If this occurs, it adds additional adolescent identity losses to his burden.

- May regress to an earlier grief stage.

- Without adequate preparation, likely to seek proving self through unhealthy, pseudo-adult behaviors, such as alcohol/drug exploration or sexual promiscuity to fill or numb the loss of a loved one, dropping out of school, running away from home.

- If the youth is driving, he may be more prone to accidents caused by impulsive risk-taking, daydreaming about his loss while driving, lack of sleep, attempts to meet multiple demands and appointments.

- If the adopted adolescent is unable to integrate traits of both the birth and the adoptive parents, to discover a unique identity, he may mimic an internal image of the birth parents. The more he knows about the biological parents, the better he can be supported in making wholesome choices about who they are. If little is known about the biological parents, the adolescent may need outside support to help grieve "missing parts" that may never be filled.

Considerations to help a grieving middle adolescent

- Recognize the crippling effects of the loss on personal emotional and social skills.

- Be alert to behavioral, social, and physical signs of grief. This age group typically does not share what they are going through or how they are feeling, because developmentally they are beginning to separate from the family and move toward peer support. (Unfortunately, peers often quickly tire of the grief process and want their friend to "get on with it," which increases the sense of isolation.)

- Monitor and adapt academic demands as the grief process naturally waxes and wanes.

- Monitor high-risk behavior, which indicates decreased judgment, attention, and concentration. When necessary, set appropriate limits that have practical consequences. For example, if the adolescent has a driver's license, it may be advisable to monitor his driving privileges by setting appropriate limits and consequences. This allows him freedom within responsible driving boundaries and may help curb driving fast, not paying attention, and/or releasing tension by impulsive judgments behind the wheel.

- Adolescence is a diurnal time in physiological development, making it difficult to get to sleep at a "reasonable hour." Monitor sleep patterns (increased difficulty getting to sleep, staying asleep, waking early). Possibly change the first class to one hour later. Also introduce mild, safe sleep aids such as the Mary Poppins Milk Recipe (see Appendix 3), or aromatherapy for sleep and relaxation.

- Adolescence is already a highly stressful time with cognitive/academic, hormonal changes, emotional and social demands of peer group. The increased stress due to loss can compromise his immune system. It is important to monitor his increased susceptibility to illness and seek appropriate medical support in a timely manner.

CHAPTER 12

LATE ADOLESCENCE
(AGES 17 TO MID-TWENTIES)

Photo by John Schoenwalter

BRIAN'S STORY: DEATH OF A CLOSE FRIEND

Brian and Jason lived in the same neighborhood, were in the same classes at school, played on the same teams in sports (soccer, football, hockey). For many years, they were inseparable, best buddies, sharing activities and confidences. Their childhoods were woven together, and their families. They even planned to room together this autumn away at college.

Then Jason died. He was driving home with his sister from a family reunion when they were hit by a drunk driver. They both died instantly. The rhythm of Brian's world died that day.

So many of Brian's hidden regulators included Jason: constant cell-phone conversations and text-messaging, weekly practice in sports along with the games, weekend activities, preparation for college in the fall. The sound of Jason's deep belly laugh; the smell reminders—especially in their rumblings and sports play, and when they shared their favorite foods; visual reminders (empty seat in class; absence on the soccer field, football field, ice arena, his smile, his gestures); Jason's physical interaction throughout the day (pats, shoves, play). The days' schedules were embedded with Jason's memories, constant reminders of his death. A deep, visceral loss. Brian felt fractured. No one person would be able to replace Jason. It would take many.

On top of that, Brian was left with gnawing questions: *Where do I put the anger from the accident? How do I even begin to fill my shattered dreams? Who am I now without my best friend?*

COGNITIVE, EMOTIONAL, AND PHYSICAL CONSIDERATIONS: USEFUL CHECKLISTS

General developmental tasks

- Aligns vocational plans and goals with personal interests and talents.

- Thinks of how he will leave home, and what he will do in life.

- Develops and accomplishes goals independently.

- Increased sophistication in social skills and interpersonal relationships.

- Exploration of "special relationships" between intimate partners.

- More spontaneous capacity for appropriate behavior in situations that require judgment, weighing alternatives and consequences, decision-making.

- A relatively solid sense of personal identity and stable personality.

- College can serve as a moratorium on adulthood, postponing some of these decisions and responsibilities; at the same time, allowing the young adult the opportunity to live away from home, while still relying on parents emotionally and financially.

Typical problems from a loss as a young adult

- Disruption in academic functioning, which could be critical if the next step (college, vocational school, etc.) depends on grades and foundational academic skills.

- The shaping of personal identity can be disrupted—developmental drive toward independence/separation (or pushing it too quickly) can become more complicated.

- Secondary losses due to a sense of isolation from peers, and restructuring schedule to fit new family demands (e.g. job to support family finances, increased care giving for younger siblings).

- Intellectualizes to avoid emotions.

- If risk-taking in middle childhood continues into late adolescence, continue to monitor the young adult's behavior closely, especially anything of frequency and intensity; such as alcohol or drug use, high-risk sexual behavior, inappropriate risk-taking in driving, sports or leisure activities.

- If adopted, this is a high-risk time for a female who may attempt to fill her emotional void by becoming pregnant. Doing so may be experienced as a "re-enactment" of the primary loss (i.e. "Someone abandoned me during adolescence. In getting pregnant, I would never abandon my baby.").

- If adopted, new losses of moving away to college or one's own apartment can create a sense of impending separation, triggering earlier losses, thereby increasing the young adult's anxiety and fears.

- If adopted, the earlier loss may be unresolved, preventing the young person from establishing intimate relationships as an adult. If this occurs, it may be advisable to seek professional therapeutic support, because it is difficult to let go of pain and create new dreams while respecting past memories, without addressing the emotions, beliefs, and visceral sensations surrounding the loss.

Considerations to help a grieving young adult

- Support endeavors at school, on the job, in her developing and expanding interests and talents.

- Help her use increased abstract reasoning for coping with life's stressors.

- Support her in using abstract reasoning to look at the loss from various perspectives, offering a deeper, more comprehensive understanding surrounding the loss.

- Be aware of the typical adolescent/young adult "leisure" activities, because some are quite dangerous. Recognize the statement by William Glaser, developer of Reality Therapy and Choice Theory: "With freedom comes responsibility." Recognize her ability to handle emerging independence, personal strengths, and weaknesses. Adjust boundaries when and where necessary. Support the youth in problem-solving risky and/or conflictual social situations.

- If adopted, moving to college or her own apartment can increase anxiety and fear. If a parent or sibling was lost, the young adult may worry that the family will be alright when she is away. Discuss the parameters of how she will leave, continued communication via cell phone, internet, visits while away, along with ways in which she can and will return home periodically (e.g. weekends, holidays, vacations, times of crisis/support). The time duration in which the adolescent is not with the family still provides her with opportunities to reunite with family members for "emotional refuelling." This opportunity to "catch up" with each others' lives allows for reconnecting with the family "hidden regulators"—physically, emotionally, and spiritually. Identifying hidden regulators via objects, food, activities, which she can take to college will help to keep her physiologically regulated while away from home.

- If adopted, the latter part of late adolescence (mid-twenties) can be a healthy time to begin searching for her birth parents or country of origin. Searching can help a young adult understand fears and to clarify expectations. As an adopted parent, give clear behavioral and verbal messages that the young person is and always will be your son or daughter and an essential part of your family.

- If you are an adoptive parent, clarify how and when you recommend that the adolescent leave home and develop a personal life as an individual, what your relationship will be like afterwards, and what support you will provide. This discussion may be repetitive, and start as young as 13...or whenever she shows signs of concern. Discuss to the degree of age comprehension based on mental and emotional development. The more the young person can anticipate and problem-solve before actual separation from the home environment, the more in control she will feel.

CONCLUSION

Hope is the thing with feathers—That perches in the soul.—Emily Dickinson

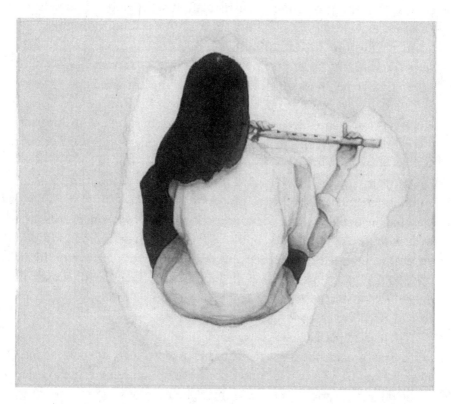

Drawing by Nol Meyer

You may feel a bit overwhelmed with the idea that childhood grief has such a long recovery process. The thought that a young child may suffer until young adulthood may grip at your heart. It would be easier to stay in denial and to dismiss the facts. But you would not be reading this book if you had not asked "How can I genuinely be helpful to this young person?"

A positive way of looking at this long journey to healing a child's grief is to recognize that young children must be able to digest their loss at their own cognitive level, so they won't be overwhelmed and "fight, flight, or freeze." Your gift to the child is rebuilding a gradual absorption of all the loss essentials. With your wholesome support, he will be able to tolerate intense feelings that occasionally arise and to practice coping skills. In neuropsychology, this practice is termed, "stress inoculation." Over time, repeated exposure to manageable stressors, supported by the presence of a reassuring caregiver, can help to strengthen the roots of the child's developing emotional self-regulation skills, and the cumulative experiences will help to build a socio-emotional foundation for stress resistance (Schore 2003a, 2003b).

All significant losses take one on a quest to understand *why*. Young children often begin by attempting to recover the lost loved one. In Larry Shles' story *Hugs and Shrugs: The Continuing Saga of a Tiny Owl Named Squib*, Squib has lost a core piece of himself and goes in search of the missing piece (i.e. inner peace). The journey to healing one's grief is never easy and, as in many children's tales, is fraught with emotional suffering. Learning to accept life's agonies allows a child's peace to arise from within, recreating the ability to love and trust again.

Like the owl in Valiska Gregory's story *Through the Mickle Woods*, the weaver must use all of the child's experiences, beliefs, emotions, and visceral feelings ("things chosen and things not") to "weave" the child's story so that, when his story is pulled round him, it will be filled with all the colors—colors of woe and colors of gladness—creating an internal core of strength, courage, and compassion.

There is no perfect map for managing a child's loss. The child brings to his grief process the ingredients of his own life: age, previous experiences, strengths, weaknesses, and resources that can support the journey of healing the grief. The main ingredient, however, to the child successfully recovering is your sensitivity and availability throughout this long and enduring process.

To heal childhood grief, the essential ingredients are the developmental tasks at each of the various stages of the young life, which address the child's grief at a level and in a way he can understand. To minimize the intense problems associated with grief, as a baker allows dough to rise in the right timing—allow your child to mature through each developmental stage.

Healing a child's grief cannot be rushed, dismissed, or ignored. The belief that you can stop support at any point is false. The child negotiates this difficult process until maturity.

Pediatric neuropsychology is an emerging science. We don't yet know if what a child missed during a developmental stage can be captured at a later date. So, better to err on the side of caution and to address the developmental tasks where we do know what occurs in each stage of a child's life.

When we read on a box, "Fragile. Handle With Care," we know there are fragile items inside, so we take extra precaution to ensure that the contents will remain safe and whole, rather than damaged and broken. On the journey of healing grief, a child is fragile and needs constancy, wisdom, and love to recapture feeling safe and to grow into a whole and stable adult.

It is what's going on inside of a child that is essential to observe and attend. Thus, this gentle reminder:

Fragile. Handle with Care.

THERAPEUTIC ACTIVITIES

The following techniques can assist any parent, caregiver or clinician in addressing a child's, or adolescent's loss to help him find a way to heal and to have a happy and healthy life. The measures are safe-and-sound approaches to meeting the neuropsychobiological needs of anyone who has lost a loved one, whether through death or adoption or some other loss in life. Many of the techniques are designed to access both right and left hemispheres as well as the limbic areas of the brain. The goal is to create intercommunication links throughout the brain and body to facilitate the healing process.

MASSAGE

There are many reasons for utilizing infant massage techniques for infants, toddlers, and preschoolers who have lost or been separated from a significant caregiver. Researchers are finding that massage can help promote better sleep, relieve colic, strengthen a young child's immune system, enhance motor skills and intellectual development.

The sense of touch is one of the most advanced abilities at birth, although not fully developed. Touch plays a surprisingly strong role in the overall quality of a child's brain development, by providing enriching experiences through tactile sensations. Massage can release pent-up muscles and reduce cortisol (see Glossary) levels that increase during the day due to changes in routine, caregivers, and environment. Massage can regulate digestion and ease congestion. Most of all, positive touch is essential for developing attachment.

When

Two to three times daily (as part of a morning ritual, possible naptime ritual, and during bath/bedtime ritual)—but not right after feeding.

Massage is also helpful when an infant experiences pain, which manifests by sudden, intense, higher-pitched, punctuated, breath-holding cries. Infants react more to pain when they are alert, hungry, or fatigued. If you are not in a place, or lack the time, to do a massage, try holding, swaddling, gently stroking, rocking, or jiggling. These can be effective in reducing an infant's reaction to pain. Allow 10–15 minutes for massage.

Technique

Place the infant/toddler on a blanket or towel. If the room is cool, be sure the blanket or towel is warm, because you will be removing the clothing. (Note: If the massage is for a preschooler, you can use a soft blanket or bed; light, loose clothing may remain on.)

It is best not to lay the child under direct sunlight or overhead light, because this can be uncomfortable and hinder his ability to relax.

Wash your hands and remove jewelry (so you won't scratch the infant). Warm a few drops of scented plant or vegetable oil, oils that are easily absorbed in the skin and are digestible should your infant suck a thumb. Scents can vary, including vanilla, almond, lavender, jasmine. Enjoy varying the scents during the day; babies enjoy the novelty.

Begin with the legs and feet, using slow, gentle strokes. If your baby splays the fingers or toes, or avoids your gaze, s/he may be telling you your touch is too deep and is stressing. A clenched fist or foot, or constriction in any area of the body indicates he is not ready to be touched there—*so don't touch there.*

It is important to be sensitive to how your infant is receiving the massage. Remain very observant of his body language, and be prepared to stop if you see any distress or cries. Just follow the infant's cues. It will be more relaxing and comforting for you, too.

During the massage, sing soft, soothing, rhythmic songs or have soft, relaxing music playing in the background. The massage should be relaxing for both the infant/toddler *and* you, the massager.

To create a gentle transition, if the massage follows a bath or precedes bedtime, you may wrap the infant in a slightly warmed towel or warmed pajamas.

PUZZLE TECHNIQUE

This technique can be utilized for all ages and can extend all through one's lifespan. If it is used to identify hidden regulators for a 0- to 3-year-old preverbal child, the caregiver (and those close to the child) will have to be the one(s) to help identify her hidden regulators. After age four, this technique can be introduced directly to the child, because he has acquired sufficient language to process questions and responses.

Areas of application

This technique can be used to:

- identify hidden regulators after a loss

- identify significant memories (positive and negative) of a loss object, pet, person, event (this objective is also helpful in identifying "ancestral stories" as well as for children who have experienced dysfunctional parenting and traumas)

- identify what a loss meant, reverberations of the loss, and how it has impacted the child's life; these memories are woven into the child's unique story (the Rock Technique, described on pp.141–147, can be used as a concrete prop for this springboard into further exploration)

- identify "shattered dreams," which unfold throughout the developmental years.

Steps

1. Parent or child brings in a picture of a person, pet, object, or situation.

2. Picture is scanned into color photocopy (or black and white). If the photo is in color, a color photocopy is preferred.

3. Therapist/caregiver draws lines on the back of the photocopy to create number of puzzle pieces for the child. With the child, you cut the picture into equal puzzle piece parts, depending on the issue and cognitive level of the child. Older children and adolescents can be instructed as to how many pieces to cut for themselves. (Note: Some parents and clinicians wonder if cutting the picture will be more painful than helpful. In my experience, children and adolescents already feel that parts of their lives were shattered by their loss. The cutting becomes a form of attunement—recognizing their pain. However, if a child does feel uncomfortable with the cutting, fold the picture rather than cut it.) *Rule of Thumb* for number of pieces in puzzle: a) Small children below age 6: 2 to 3 puzzle pieces. b) Elementary age children (ages 6 – 11): 4 to 5 puzzle pieces. c) Adolescents and above: 5 to 8 puzzle pieces. No more than 8 pieces should ever be used for the

Puzzle Technique as it becomes too many pieces to negotiate within the activity.

4. One piece at a time. The child selects one piece, and turns it over with the therapist. You ask the child questions based on her cognitive/ emotional developmental level as well as the issue you are exploring. For example, when identifying the hidden regulators of a four-year-old who lost her father, ask the child *What do you miss most about Daddy?* On the back of each puzzle piece, write the child's response in one color of ink (you can allow the child to select the color). Continue this process until all three or four pieces are completed.

5. After the pieces have responses written on them, return to each piece and ask *Who would you like to do this now for you or with you?* Using a different color (which again the child may be allowed to choose), write the child's response below the previous question and response.

6. Depending on time and the child's attention span, return to each puzzle piece and ask *When and how many times a day or week should this happen?* Again, write the response on the back of each puzzle piece, using a third color to designate the question/response.

7. The puzzle pieces are then shared with the caregiver(s) as part of the Action Plan. Often, these people are invited into the session as supportive observers. Encourage the child to share the information written on the puzzle pieces, as this can offer her a sense of control and empowerment in this process. The caregivers are critical parts of the Action Plan, and this is the time to identify strengths and weaknesses (blocks, resistances, potential problems, and availability of others the child wants to carry out: "Who can do it for you?"). This part of the activity is essential to ensure a successful follow-through of the Plan.

8. Scan the puzzle information into the computer (both front and back). You keep the copy. Let the child take the pieces with her to implement during the weeks ahead. These pieces are "transitional objects" between you and the child, as well as concrete objects to help her remember the session better.

9. In the follow-up session, the child brings back the puzzle piece. You and the child (along with caregivers) discuss each piece as to how it is working and what needs to be revised. The child's Action Plan continues to be tweaked as necessary—reviewed, evaluated, and revised as necessary.

For shattered dreams, stories, memories

Ask a variety of questions, that may include the child's thoughts and feelings (i.e. visceral sensations in the various sensory modalities), beliefs, and emotions that surrounded each part of the story, memory, or piece of the lost expectations (shattered dreams) (e.g. *Tell me what dreams you had that were shattered by the loss of ___?*).

Each piece is a response to a dream that was shattered (and written in a color chosen by the child).

Next questions (using different colors for each question) can include: *What thoughts do you have around ___?* Specify the response to the identified "shattered" aspect. *What feelings surround this identified shattered aspect? What would this look like if the dream were still alive? What would it sound like? What would it feel like? What would it smell like? What would the actions/behaviors be like, etc.? How might you be able to fill this dream now?*

Identifying hidden regulators with older children and adolescents

Ask more detailed questions, probing for sensory modalities (sounds, smells, tastes, visuals, tactile sensations) that were involved in the identified rituals, routines, and activities they identified on their puzzle pieces.

THE ROCK TECHNIQUE

The intent of the rock techniques is to create a coherent experience (thoughts, emotions, feelings/sensations) during the process. There are three ways to use the Rock Technique, all of which help light up and stimulate the left hemisphere (language processing), right hemisphere (emotional, relational, sensory processing) and subcortical (limbic—emotional processing), as well as one's bodily sensations.

I. The Stone Child—Ancestral stories inherited by the child and/or child's current story, as told through the rock

OBJECTIVE

The rock is used to validate the child's life story or life situation. This technique is to be introduced *only* when you have sufficiently understood the child's life story and the potential lessons and/or generational inherited stories which the child is exhibiting (re-enacting) in his life. The rock technique in this activity can be utilized to support the child/adolescent's understanding of his story as well as an encouragement of commitment to change aspects which are creating suffering for him. *Note that this particular technique can only be utilized infrequently (once every six to eight months) during the therapeutic process.*

The therapist is to find two or three rocks through which she or he is able to tell (illustrate) portions of the child's story/journey. Offer only these rocks to the child in the activity. The rocks should be symbolic of the child's life story or situation. For example, a rock which has varying layered colors or varying level color changes can be representative of different years in the child's life. Rocks which have darker colors at one end with rough edges or indentations can be symbolic of early wounds/trauma. Indentations or rough edges midway in a rock might be symbolic of wounds/loss/trauma which occurred midway in his life. In other words, the therapist utilizes the physical attributes of the rock to illustrate the child's situation and/or life story.

In the telling of a child's story via the rock, the rock now offers the child the following: (a) an affirmation of his story/situation; (b) the affirmation helps encourage and support the child's motivation to take part in a particular technique/strategies designed to help alleviate his suffering; and (c) the rock becomes a transitional object, holding the energy and memories of the adult/child's time together.

The Rock Technique works well with children who still are at an emotional reasoning level of "magical thinking" about their story/loss/situation. Magical thinking is the erroneous belief that one's thoughts, words, or actions will cause or prevent a specific outcome in some way that defies commonly understood laws of cause and effect. Magical thinking is a normal part of child development for the ages two to nine. However, older children who have suffered an early loss may still be using magical thinking in their reasoning about the loss. At this reasoning level, the rock is also used as a transitional object of the therapeutic relationship between the therapist and the child.

Once the child has chosen his rock, save the other rock(s) which you had initially selected and which could also illustrate the child's story/situation. Place this in the child's file to be offered should he lose his initial chosen rock. I have found that when such children lose their rock, it can trigger an increased sense of loss, shame, and/or guilt. The opportunity to offer him another rock which could also illustrate his story helps (a) "fill" the emptiness and subsequent feelings around the loss while (b) allowing him a concrete experience whose hidden meaning infers something like: "Although this cannot replace the rock you chose to support you (i.e. as no one can replace the one you lost), it also has aspects which resemble your story/journey and thus might be helpful (i.e. willingness to allow another to be available and supportive in their healing journey)."

The Rock Technique in this activity is offered around the last 15 minutes of a session. It is initiated after a discussion of thoughts, feelings, and behaviors regarding a particular situation/issue has occurred and a strategy identified which the child is motivated to implement (practice).

TECHNIQUE: PART I

The therapist can begin the activity by offering a brief comment to the child such as: "You've chosen a strategy to try to see if it can help with _____ (i.e. identify the current situation, feelings, emotion, or /behaviors). Let's be a little playful before the end of our time today. Okay?"

Ask the child to close his eyes and feel for the rock that will best support him in practicing these new thoughts, behaviors, and/or feelings. For example: "Close your eyes and feel for the rock that will help you remember to _____." "Close your eyes and feel for the rock that will give you the strength/courage to _____."

Requesting the child to close his eyes and feel for the rock that will best support him in identifying the particular behavior or situation being addressed allows the child to access his bodily sensations (i.e. feelings). If the child's eyes were open, he would be less focused on his bodily sensations and preverbal messages. In this activity, keeping the eyes open would increase the potential of thinking cognitively about what rock he liked best vs. respecting his preverbal connections (i.e. feelings) which need to be acknowledged. Once these feelings are consciously accessible, these preverbal connections are followed by the verbal, mental explanation of his story. The grieving process needs to access the feeling levels in order for the child to be comfortable with his feelings. This technique is a way to allow the child gradually to become more comfortable with his feelings as the activity elicits positive, supportive feelings. This can facilitate the child's growing strength in being able to move into his feelings about the loss, allowing the various feelings to be acknowledged, moved through, and discharged (no longer being blocked in the body by what the mind is thinking). Thus, closing the eyes affords the child a gentle way of becoming more familiar and comfortable with his feeling states, without the feelings becoming overwhelming and overarousing.

Then, hand the child one rock at a time, making sure that he feels the rock with the left hand, the right hand, and then with both hands. (In doing so, you are ensuring that the child is accessing the right hemisphere, left hemisphere, limbic, and body areas, thereby opening up all these areas during the process. It is a nice way to incorporate and utilize the body–mind connection.)

Use no more than three to four rocks in this activity (a maximum of three for children under age 11). By the end of Part I, the child will have selected a rock that feels the most appropriate for the problem/task he will work on.

TECHNIQUE: PART 2

Tell the child the story of the rock (i.e. point out the various aspects of the rock, which remind you of the child's story). For example:

- If you tell the story from a developmental perspective, rocks with various hues and layers can signify various sequential times and events in the child/adolescent's life.

- If you want to share a rock that symbolizes specific wounding, select a rock with indentations, mildly sharp edges in parts, deep coloring, or bubbles in middle parts, etc.

- If you want a rock that symbolizes shattered dreams or feelings of fragmentation, select a rock with a variety of freckles, spots, or circles in which it is hard to find any specific cohesiveness in an area of the rock.

Overall, what is essential is your ability to find rocks that the child feels he can successfully use, which validates his own story. (It is also important to find rocks that have color and light, as well as layers or areas that may symbolize hope and strength, in addition to wounding aspects in a rock.)

II. How heavy is my baggage? My behaviors are increasing my load

PREMISE

A child's story consists not only of mental but also emotional memories—old emotions that are being revived continuously. Eckhart Tolle (2005) wrote:

> As in the case of the monk who carried the burden of his resentment for five hours by feeding it with high thought, most people carry a large amount of unnecessary baggage, both mental and emotional, throughout their lives. They limit themselves through grievances, regret, hostility, guilt. Their emotional thinking has become their self, and so they hang on to the old emotions because it strengthens their identity... What a heavy burden of past they carry around with them in their minds. (p.139)

OBJECTIVE

To allow the child to *feel* the weight of his behavior. These are children who tend to (1) act without thinking, or (2) dismiss the significance of their behaviors, thus minimizing the effect on others. Once you decide to use this technique in a session, in the week prior give the child a cartoon that states something like the

Ziggy cartoon: "In this journey through a life filled with emotional baggage, it sure would be nice to only have a carry-on."

In sessions, I sometimes tell the child-client that we don't always know what baggage is in our suitcases until we add new baggage by our behaviors; that we sometimes have to do a "behavioral autopsy"—look closely at our behaviors in order to better understand the heaviness of our emotional and behavioral baggage.

TECHNIQUE: PART 1

Have different sizes and weights of rocks readily accessible in the office. As the child is describing how his week has gone, hand him a rock based on the intensity/frequency/duration of the maladaptive behavior that has been hindering his ability to be in the world. When handing a rock to the child, say nothing (no verbalizations). Listen and observe how congruent the child is as he shares behaviors (i.e. observe for signs of insight, shame, remorse, how incidents are described, etc.).

Have the child hold all the rocks in his hands (and lap if many rocks). Do not set, or allow the rocks, to be on the table or the floor, because this would symbolize displacement, projection, denial. In implementing this activity, you are acting as the "super-ego," judging the size and weight of each rock, based on how society most likely would respond (or already has responded) to the child's behavior. It is important that you *remember* which rock you give the child in relation to each behavior.

At the end of the sharing, if there are a lot of rocks, request the child to stand. The rocks should fall on the floor (perhaps onto his toes). If the rocks hit the child's body, comment: *I am so sorry that your rock hurt you* (metaphor for "your behavior hurting you"). Children who do stand when requested, often are those who have (1) poor cause–effect reasoning, (2) impulsive behavior, or (3) do what they are told without questioning adults and peers, which can put them in harm's way.

If a child refuses to stand, knowing the rocks will fall and he could get hurt or will have to pick them up, cause-and-effect is intact at a concrete level of reasoning. Say something like, *Absolutely, you have the ability to think ahead when you are in a calm emotional state. Our goal is to get you to a place where you will be able to access this good reasoning whenever you really need it. Whenever you are really stressed.*

TECHNIQUE: PART 2

Ask the child to select a rock he wishes to work with for that session. It can be any size and weight. Let the child decide what he is motivated to deal with at this time (energy/investment). This is also the rock he is willing to trust you to work with. (*Note:* If the child is successful in reducing the size of the current rock pile, by successful problem-solving, he will be more likely to select larger rocks when you implement this technique again. You must be able to remember what story/behavior goes with which rock.) The child then puts the rock on the table between him and you.

Never take the rock from the child, because that is a message that you have "taken the monkey off his back" and that you now will carry the child's load. Placing the rock on the table between you is a symbol of dyadic attachment in sharing and problem-solving.

Now discuss the child's behavior *through* the rock *in third person* to help the child perceive with a greater perspective and greater objectivity, while reducing the possibility of toxic shame or guilt and emotional collapses during the process. Direct questions toward gaining more information around the following: (1) antecedents (i.e. sounds/statements, smells, visual perceptions, tastes, touch, actions), (2) behaviors following antecedents (include sensory modalities), (3) consequences. Include the child's feelings, thoughts, and emotions that occur during the three phases.

Inquire as to what helped in the past and what could help now (designing a possible solution). You may offer suggestions in the solution design. The new solution should not be too complicated (i.e. multiple steps) or too novel (i.e. unfamiliar) in application. (*Note:* Feelings are visceral, bodily sensations. So ask questions about the sensory input surrounding an event: sounds, visuals, smells, tastes, and tactile sensations, and how the body felt during this time. Emotions are labels we give to the feelings and thoughts that accompany them.

Then have the child select a course of action and take the rock with him as a concrete, symbolic reminder of his Action Plan whenever the behavior recurs; it also serves as a transitional object of support and encouragement from you.

If there is a way physically to practice the new solution during the therapeutic session, that would be helpful also. For example, play a game in which the child may become mildly to moderately stressed in order to utilize the new solution during the session.

TECHNIQUE: PART 3

During the next session, the child brings the rock back. Again discuss, in third person, how the Action Plan is working with the rock.

The child may exchange it for a lighter rock if the solution was successful, or may keep it and be given another, lighter rock—an indication that the "baggage" is being reduced (i.e. the child's ability to be successful in dealing with his problems/issues). Many young clients like to see their rocks become smaller.

III. Rock adjunct to Pebble Technique

This very concrete adjunct to the Pebble Technique (described on pp.99–101) can be utilized when the pebble makes a splash and hits a nerve. This technique allows the child to talk about his fears without turning the spotlight directly on himself. The child selects a simple pebble or colorful rock which you (clinician/caregiver) can place between you. Discussing the pebble in third person allows the child some distance from his fears, offering an opportunity to share thoughts and feelings while you begin exploring the reality-testing facts and make suggestions. The child then places the rock in a special box, jewelry bag, or pouch, symbolizing that it is being worked upon (without being thrown away, abandoned).

AROMATHERAPY

Plants contain a wide variety of chemicals and medicinal properties in unique combinations that have healing effects as well as subtle-energetic effects upon the human body. Aromas (scents) go directly from the olfactory bulb to the amygdala, the only sensory modality with such a direct line. Because the aroma of essential oils affects the amygdala and pineal gland in the brain, it can help the mind and body by soothing and calming emotional trauma. The aromatic molecules of the essential oil are absorbed into the bloodstream from the nasal cavity to the limbic system. They activate the amygdala (memory center for fear and trauma), and sedate and relax the sympathetic/parasympathetic system.

There are a variety of aromas that address body, emotions, and thoughts. Aromatherapy can be introduced through multiple mediums. For example: on wrists similar to perfume and cologne (be sure the oil is not an irritant to the skin); on sweat bands, handkerchiefs, scarves, where one has easy access to the scent; in water fountains, so one has the aroma as well as the sound of flowing water; in bath water, which relaxes the body through skin conduction (the warmth as well as the aroma stays with the child throughout the night). There are also soaps and lotions with various aromas, so they are immediately on the hands. Scents can be put on blankets, stuffed animals, etc., as part of a hidden regulator during separation. There are aroma doughs to use with children to calm them down through the olfactory and touch senses. Children/adolescents and caregivers often have wonderful ideas of ways to access aromas that will fit their environmental situation and not be intrusive or distracting.

Some essential oils and their properties:

- *Basil:* May be beneficial for mental fatigue. May stimulate and sharpen sense of smell.

- *Bergamot:* Has about 300 chemical constituents that contribute refreshing mood-lifting qualities.

- *Cedarwood:* Recognized historically for its calming, purifying properties. Also helps to calm nervous tension.

- *Chamomile (roman, German):* May be used as a subtle sedative action. Because it is calming and relaxing, it can help combat depression, insomnia, and stress. It has been used to eliminate some of the emotional charge of anxiety, irritability, and nervousness, dispel anger, stabilize the emotions, and help to release emotions linked to the past.

- *Clary sage:* Used to help balance the extremes of emotions and restores emotional equilibrium; alleviates melancholy and lifts depression. In the nervous system, it is used to ease fear and nervousness, increase concentration, and stimulate mental activity without being overstimulating. In stressful situations, clary sage oil is used to reduce deep-seated tension, slow a racing mind, calm nerves, reduce irritability, anxiety, and feelings of panic.

- *Coriander:* Researched in animal studies at Cairo University. Has soothing and calming properties.

- *Fir, Douglas:* Is spiritually realigning.

- *Frankincense:* Frankincense is now being researched and used therapeutically in European and American hospitals. Stimulating and elevating to the mind; helps in overcoming stress and despair.

- *Geranium:* Its strength lies in its ability to revitalize tissue. It is excellent for the skin, and its aromatic influence helps to release negative memories.

- *Ginger:* Warming, stimulating, and grounding. It aids memory; in the nervous system it can help with nervous exhaustion, tiredness. Emotionally it is used to aid memory, warms cold, flat emotions, and sharpens senses.

- *Goldenrod:* Relaxing and calming effects. Good for stomach problems, upsets.

- *Grapefruit:* May help diminish depression, headache, and performance stress, jet lag, PMS, alcohol and drug withdrawal. Can be emotionally uplifting and energizing. *Warning:* If there is any possibility of a seizure disorder, it is recommended that one not use this scent.

- *Jasmine:* Uplifting and stimulating. Jasmine has been historically used for attraction, romance, and balancing the feminine body of energy.

- *Juniper:* Used to support proper nerve function.

- *Lavender:* Therapeutic-grade lavender is highly regarded for skin. Lavender has been clinically evaluated for its relaxing effects. It may be used to cleanse cuts, bruises, and skin irritations. The fragrance is calming, relaxing, and balancing—physically and emotionally.

- *Ledum:* As a tea, ledum soothes stomachs, coughs, and hoarseness. It is also believed to calm occasional nervousness.

- *Lemon:* Relieves mental fatigue, improves mental clarity and alertness, sharpens the senses, reduces stress, balancing and calming, energizing.

- *Lemongrass:* Used as an antidepressant, to soothe aches and pains, and to relieve stress.

- *Lime:* Cheering and restorative, lime refreshes a tired mind. Like lemon, can sharpen the sense, reduce stress, calm the body, and energize the mind.

- *Mandarin:* One of children's favorite oils, it calms excitations, muscle spasms, and cramps. Can be used as a mild sedative for disrupted sleep.

- *Marjoram:* Assists in calming the nerves. Good for sleep disorders.

- *Myrrh:* It has one of the highest levels of sesquiterpenses, a class of compounds with direct effects on the hypothalamus, pituitary, and the Limbic system, the seat of emotions.

- *Orange:* Brings peace and happiness to the mind and body. Uplifting and elevating.

- *Peppermint:* Has the ability to directly affect the brain's satiety center, which triggers a sensation of fullness after meals. Also alerting, calming, and helpful with stomach problems.

- *Rose:* Helps bring balance and harmony. Is stimulating and elevating to the mind, creating a sense of well-being.

- *Rosemary:* Helps to overcome mental fatigue.

- *Rosewood:* May bring a feeling of stability and grounding. Helps to up-lift feelings of despair.

- *Sandalwood:* Researched in Europe for its ability to oxygenate a part of the brain known as the pineal gland, part of the Limbic system. The pineal gland is responsible for releasing melatonin, which enhances deep sleep.

- *Spearmint:* May help open and release emotional blocks and bring about a feeling of balance.

- *Spruce:* Helps to open and release emotional blocks, bringing about a feeling of balance. May also bring about a feeling of peaceful security.

- *Tangerine:* Helps with occasional nervous irritability. An excellent oil to help uplift the spirit and bring about a sense of security.

- *Tarragon:* Can be used as a mild sedative, digestive aid, and as a heart disease prevention aid. It has been used to relieve stomach cramps, increase appetite, calm the nerves, and decrease fatigue. It is also used to relieve insomnia, hyperactivity, depression, and nervous exhaustion.

- *Valerian:* Used for thousands of years for its calming, grounding, and emotionally balancing influences. During the last three decades, valerian has been clinically investigated for its relaxing properties. Researchers have pinpointed the sesquiterpenses, valerenic acid and valerone, as the active constituents that exert a calming effect on the central nervous system.

- *Vetiver:* One of the oils that is highest in sesquiterpenses, vetiver has been studied for improving children's behavior. May help one cope with stress and recover from emotional trauma and shock.

- *Wintergreen:* May help soothe head tension when used as a massage oil.

- *Ylang ylang:* May be extremely effective in calming and bringing about a sense of relaxation. Often used in men's fragrances.

Some conditions and concerns, and the essential oils that may be beneficial:

- *Abuse (physical and emotional):* Geranium, sandalwood, and melissa are aromas that affect the limbic system where implicit memories are stored; these aromas can help release pent-up trauma, emotions, and memories.

- *Anger:* Bergamot, cedarwood, roman chamomile, frankincense, lavender, lemon, marjoram, orange, rose, sandalwood.

- *Anorexia:* Tarragon, mandarin, orange, lemon, ginger (directly impact the limbic system; when inhaled regularly, along with psychotherapy, can combat the emotional symptom).

- *Anxiety:* Orange, roman chamomile, lavender, cedarwood.

- *Attention/focus:* Lemon, lime, orange, lemongrass, grapefruit, basil, peppermint, rosemary, ylang ylang (helps balance serotonin, improves brain function for ADHD).

- *Emotional trauma* that disrupts stomach and digestive system: Frankincense, lavender, lemon, rose, valerian, German chamomile.

- *Impaired concentration:* Basil, lemon, peppermint, bergamot, rosemary, clary sage, frankincense.

- *Mental fatigue:* Rosemary, cedarwood, peppermint, frankincense.

STRESS BALLS

Stress balls are a tangible tool to provide tension release and teach deep breathing and mindful relaxation. One resource for a variety of stress balls is: Pocket Full of Therapy, P.O. Box 174, 732.441.0404, www.pfot.com. However, stress balls are found in most sensory processing catalogs. One can also find various balls that can be used for stress, by browsing through grocery stores, children's toy sections in department stores, and various children's toy centers. Following are just a few found in sensory catalogs:

- *Inside-Out Ball:* Change the soft, smooth ball into a spiky ball. Experience: stretchy, prickly; smooth, soft.

- *Ergo Balls:* Soft yet tactile, resistive yet yielding, amazingly comforting. Made with a cotton Lycra-cover filled with specially coated plastic beads that glide smoothly over each other. The result is a squeezable, hand exerciser and stress-relief tool.

- *Schrunchins:* Squeezable animals or balls made of memory foam. Give them a squeeze and watch them unscrunch and change right before your eyes. Animals and balls are assorted.

- *Mini Stretchy String:* Made from the most elastic compound, these half-inch long strings stretch like crazy. Six colorful strings per pack. Tie them together, wrap them around fingers, twirl them in the air or tie them to wrist as a handy fidget. Each strand provides over eight feet of stretchy fun.

STORYTELLING

Storytelling is a wonderful, indirect way to deal with difficult subjects. Stories can help us consider new ways to deal with our predicaments in our lives. Most stories have both good and evil in their characters.

Remember the story of Oliver Twist? It is the story of an orphan, the loss of maternal care, and subsequent abusive caregivers. The story shows a child's creativity and resilience in living through difficult times.

Through stories (and movies) we connect with others, and share worlds, thoughts, and feelings of the characters. Stories provide the opportunity for moral lessons, self-reflection, and emotional outlets (thanks to those lovely, yet powerful, mirror neurons). Cozolino (2002) wrote:

> Narratives allow us to place ourselves within the story. Through these stories, we have the opportunities to ponder ourselves in an objective way within an infinite number of contexts. We can escape our bodies and the present moment in imagination to create other possible selves, ways of being, and worlds that have yet to be created. (p.35)

Storytelling is good for the developing brain, because it requires the brain to sustain attention, remember the plot, keep track of time and sequences, while stimulating connection to our visceral feelings and emotions while listening, reading, or watching a character's facial expressions, postures, movements, and emotions. Through all of this, the right and left hemispheres are accessed, allowing for "integration of a wide variety of neural networks" (Siegel 1999).

Stories offer a large realm of material from which to draw: myths, fables, legends, epics, parables, ballads, anecdotes, folklore, fairy tales, news and magazine stories, and film. We can select stories that have "positive, pleasant" outcomes (i.e. ending in the left hemisphere), or ones that have "negative, unpleasant" outcomes (i.e. ending in the right hemisphere).

Sufi tales are short tales that tend to end in the left hemisphere, offering a bit of humor to the moral of the story. Aesop's fables tend to be short and end more with the right hemisphere: negative sensation, more tragic, thus the message is experienced as more severe and remembered for survival.

It just depends on what you want the child to remember the most. The large variety of story material allows professionals/caregivers to select content at the child's cognitive and emotional developmental level as well as stories that fit the child's culture and interests. As the child matures, so would the story choices, to offer an expanding perspective on the child's life loss.

Stories can range from 30 seconds to hours, offering the child the opportunity to expand her tolerance gradually to stay attentive to the content and to emotions in the grief process, without feeling the need to run away. Stories create a springboard for discussion without having to shine the spotlight directly on the child or adolescent.

Stories are a useful tool to help prime the individual's brain and body connections, in becoming more familiar and tolerant of situations and emotions (i.e. levels of arousal) in their lives which they have tended to avoid, or they have shut down. Good stories should access the positive emotions of the left hemisphere and the negative emotions of the right hemisphere, as well as descriptions of the character's bodily sensations in various situations. Stories can help the child become more familiar with observing, noticing, and attending to sensations, thoughts, and feelings, even when unpleasant or painful. Stories describe characters with an "intrapersonal attunement" to themselves, as well as characters who are intrapersonally misattuned to themselves and others—while offering solutions and consequences to each character's behavioral choices.

Stories are a wonderful and effective way to support a child or adolescent through the developmental years of her grief journey. As each new stage offers an opportunity to view the journey through expanded cognitive eyes, often triggering new thoughts and their accompanying emotions, stories can offer ways to become familiar with and handle new perceptions. Stories, thus, provide an outlet for new experiences.

TRANSITIONAL TOOLS

WINDOW CARDS

Helpful during lifestyle transitions and for inspiration. Window cards create tangible communication tools—in the form of inspiring, supporting quotes that help reinforce key messages and core values, and inspire and motivate children in creative, fun, and effective ways. There are 30 positive, optimistic, inspirational quotes in each deck. Sharing a window card with a child during his grieving process can support the nurturing of your relationship. It offers a thoughtful, attentive, and creative communication while he is away from home or between the therapeutic sessions. Window cards can be utilized in a variety of supportive ways:

- to commemorate anniversary dates

- as a transitional object to let the child know you are thinking of him until you see him again (be it a few hours, a day, a week, etc.)

- as an encouraging, concrete form to support him in his commitment to try some new strategy/technique/thought to deal with a stressful emotion or situation

- as a celebration/congratulations of an event, success in a behavior or situation, or achievement.

In addition to the inspiration quotes inside the pop-up window card, there are lines on the back of the card in which you can date when you gave it and personalize the back with your own special message. I have found that children and adolescents hold onto these cards (as they do the "story" rocks) as reminders and remembrances of our time and journey together. There are a variety of card decks for both children and adolescents/adults.

Examples of inspirational messages
CHILDREN DECKS

I'm Proud of You pop-up deck:
"Every problem is a gift. It's a chance to do your very best."
"Friends are rare. Handle with care."

I Believe in You pop-up deck:
"Oh, isn't it fun to just go ahead and do all the things that others think you won't be able to do?"

Reach for the Stars pop-up deck:
"Follow your dreams. They know the way."

ADOLESCENT/ADULT DECKS

Brilliance pop-up deck:
"Somehow, someone is looking for exactly what you have to offer."
"You are loved. If so, what else matters?"

Believe pop-up deck:
"Every day holds the possibility of a miracle."
 "All things are possible once you make them so."

Whatever It Takes pop-up deck:
"Live all you can. It's a mistake not to."

Window cards are available from Compendium, Inc. (www.compendium.com; Phone: 800-914-3327).

PAIN COMFORTERS

Tummy bags

Tummy bags can be made by family members, friends or brought from spas, health stores, or sensory-processing catalogs. Tummy bags can be used warm to calm tummy aches and to help with sleep; for headaches, use cold. Tummy bags can be scented with specific aromas depending on the child's behavior manifestation. Slip into a microwave one minute, or chill in the freezer as a cold pack. One source for tummy bags: Tummy Ache Bag by JoJo Beanyhead Company, Yellow Springs, CA 45387.

Neck pillow

Spas often have small scented pillows that can be placed in a microwave or freezer. Many occupational therapists and physiotherapists know how to make such bags and can offer advice on how to select fabric, stuffing, and weight amount for a particular child.

MARY POPPINS MILK RECIPE

Milk contains a naturally occurring amino acid called l-tryptophan, which clinical research has shown to be an effective sleep aid (Hartmann 1982). Milk, according to Daniel Amen, has been found to be helpful for improving sleep, decreasing aggressiveness, and improving mood (Amen 1998). The Mary Poppins Milk Recipe is adapted from Daniel Amen's Milk Recipe, and can be adjusted to fit the age of the child.

For children ages 2 to 5:

> ½ cup warm milk
>
> 1 teaspoon pure vanilla
>
> 1 teaspoon sugar/honey

For children 5 years and older:

> 1 cup warm milk
>
> 1 tablespoon pure vanilla
>
> 1 tablespoon sugar/honey

Before using, check with your family pediatrician to make sure the child is not allergic to this recipe. If younger than 3, always check with a pediatrician first.

GLOSSARY

Abstract reasoning: A style of thinking characterized by the ability to use concepts and to make and understand generalizations such as of the properties or patterns shared by a variety of specific items or events. Allows an individual to make and test hypotheses. Highest form of problem-solving.

Affect regulation: Regulation of one's emotions.

Amygdala: Almond-shaped structure located in the limbic area. The amygdala recognizes innate biological fears and activates relevant automatic responses for survival purposes. Known as the "fear button," it can produce fight/flight/freeze responses. The amygdala can add positive and negative emotional memories to an experience, which are subsequently used in similar situations.

Attachment: A close and meaningful relationship with another individual. It has been shown that the quality of attachment that an infant has with the mother or significant caregiver affects physical, cognitive, emotional, and social development.

Attunement: In the study of interpersonal relationships, attunement is the ability of a person to focus his or her attention on the internal world of another. For example, the ability of a caregiver to focus on his or her child's internal state enables what Siegel terms "feeling felt" by each other (Siegel 2007). The ability to focus attention on the other's internal world allows one to feel understood and thus not alone in the world. Attunement is what allows a caregiver to offer appropriate support to the child in that moment. It is the foundation for trust and empathy in relationships.

Cerebral: Referring to the cerebrum, the upper or main portion of the brain, often used to refer to the entire brain.

Concrete reasoning: A style of thinking in which the individual sees each situation as unique and separate. As such, the individual is unable to generalize from the similarities between situations. Language and perceptions are interpreted literally so that proverbs are not easily grasped. Concrete reasoning is part of normal development (ages 6 to 11 years).

Cortisol: A primary stress hormone that maintains blood pressure and produces glucose in times of stress. Mild-to-moderate cortisol levels are essential to motivation, learning, adaptation. Cortisol is the body's natural stress-fighting and anti-inflammatory hormone. However, when cortisol reaches severe levels, it becomes toxic and can cause death to developing cells, resulting in auto-immune breakdowns.

Dissociation: A psychological process involving alterations in identity or sense of self. These alterations in sense of self can include: mild and transient sense that the world or the self is "unreal" (derealization and depersonalization); more permanent states such as amnesia (loss of memory); or fugue states (a person forgets who he or she is and assumes a new identity). The most severe form known is dissociative identity disorder (formerly known as multiple personality disorder).

Explicit memory: Develops later than implicit memory. Begins to come into operation at around 18 months when the hippocampus begins to mature. Known also as declarative memory because it is organized by language related to visual images. It is the conscious organization of experiences. Explicit memory may be *episodic*—the type we use in the course of personal experiences to guide our immediate behaviors (memory of events, activities, etc.) or *semantic*—the type we use for gathering information (facts) and learning.

Gustatory: Relates to the sense of taste. Is a primary sensory modality. Taste is considered to be a chemical modality and begins to develop before birth.

Hidden regulators: Preferences for highly specific sensory features in a significant other. Hidden regulators include all the various sensory modalities: auditory, olfactory, temperature, tactile, visual, taste, movement, etc. Through hidden regulators, the mother (caregiver) maintains the level and pattern of her baby's behavior and physiology by her interactions with it. It is the abrupt loss of all these sensory regulators that results in the separation response of protest and despair. Hidden regulators are with us throughout our entire lives. As such, they must be addressed during the entire grief-recovery journey, no matter at what age the separation or loss occurs.

Hippocampus: Situated under the inner surface of the temporal lobes. Plays a key role in the formation and retrieval of long-term memories (i.e. explicit memories). In males, the hippocampus shrinks more under chronic stress. In females, the hippocampus shrinks more under acute stress. Alzheimer's disease involves the progressive degeneration of hippocampal neurons and declarative memory functions.

Implicit memory: The primary memory mode during the first three to four years of life. The behavioral patterns emerging from learned association, often termed conditioning. Implicit memory functions to enhance survival, because it is the primary source of learning and behavior, basically running on an unconscious (preverbal) level. Dominant for preverbal organization, emotional memory, sensory-motor memory, visceral memory, and procedural memory.

Kinesthetic: The sense by which motor/muscular motion and one's position in space are perceived. Kinesthetic pertains to sensations derived from muscles or movement. The kinesthetic system interprets the excursion and direction of joint movement. Considered to be one of the sensory modalities utilized in learning. Also part of hidden regulators.

Limbic system: A term used to describe various structures of the brain (including the amygdala and hippocampus) that are important in the regulation of emotion and motivation.

Maternal representation: The memories or templates that encode an infant's experiences of the mother. For example, the infant assumes that the mother it smells is the same as the mother it feels and, thus, represents the whole object. These representations are important in determining the ultimate form, function, and affective impact the child will create in developing expectations in relation to his or her attachment figures. The nonverbal groundwork for maternal representation is laid down by 12 months of age.

Mirror neurons: Known as "Monkey See, Monkey Do" neurons, because they are highly involved in imitational learning. These mirror neurons, located in the premotor and motor areas of the prefrontal cortex, parietal, occipital, temporal, insular, anterior gyrus, and Broca's areas, and most likely other areas of the cortex, become activated when one is observing a specific action in another, thinking about the action, and carrying out the same action. They are the neuronal substrate called mimicry, because one learns by mimicking what one sees being modeled. Because of our mirror neurons, we experience the thrill of watching sports as well as connecting to characters on the screen in movies. Involved in building the foundation for empathy.

Neurotransmitter: A chemical released by neurons that relays information to other cells.

Object constancy: The tendency for objects to be perceived as unchanging, despite variations in the positions in and conditions under which the objects are observed (e.g. a book's shape is always perceived as a rectangle regardless of the visual angle from which it is viewed). In psychoanalysis, object constancy refers to the relatively enduring emotional investment in another person.

Olfactory: A primary sensory modality related to the sense of smell. Begins to come into operation before birth. Part of the hidden regulators.

Pathological mourning: Significant reactions/expressions to loss which result in marked distress and duration *in excess* of what is expected in the grief process and cause significant impairment in social functioning along with marked and prolonged overall functional impairment. Insecure attachment disorders are at risk for pathological mourning during significant losses.

Preoperational reasoning: The second stage in Piaget's theory coinciding with ages two to seven when the child starts to use symbols such as language to represent objects. For instance, the child understands the word "dog" although a real dog is not seen. The preoperational reasoner learns from concrete evidence (experience) and tends to be unaware of another person's perspective. They exhibit egocentric thought and language. Trial and error reasoning is an essential component of this reasoning level.

Preverbal: Actions, experiences, memories not regulated by language. From 80 to 90 percent of our world is negotiated preverbally. For example, procedural memories are preverbal memories.

Procedural memory: Long-term memory of skills and procedures, or "how-to" knowledge. Considered an aspect of implicit memory.

Sensory-motor reasoning: Most researchers consider approximately the first two years of life to be the sensory-motor stage. It is the foundation for early learning and occurs preverbally (without language). The infant mainly makes use of his or her senses and motor capabilities to experience the environment. Sensory-motor reasoning is "thinking by doing." The sensory-motor infant gains physical and emotional knowledge of caregivers and environment through his or her sensory-motor experiences. It is predominately right hemisphere and body oriented.

Tactile: Pertains to the ability to feel objects by touch. One of the primary sensory modalities. Part of the hidden regulators.

BIBLIOGRAPHY

Abraham, K. (1912) Letter from Karl Abraham to Sigmund Freud, January 11, 1912. In E. Falzeder (2002) *The Complete Correspondence of Sigmund Freud and Karl Abraham 1907–1925*. London and New York, NY: Karnac Books, p.146.

Amen, D.G. (1998) *Change Your Brain: Change Your Life*. New York, NY: Three Rivers Press.

Anisman, H., Zahariah, M.D., Meaney, M.J. and Merali, Z. (1998) "Do early life events permanently alter behavioral and hormonal responses to stressors?" *International Journal of Developmental Neuroscience 16*, 149–164.

Benedict, R.F. (1934) *Patterns of Culture*. Boston, MA: Houghton-Mifflin.

Blume, J. (1982) *Tiger Eyes*. New York, NY: Laurel Leaf Publishers.

Bowlby, J. (1951) *Maternal Care and Mental Health*. Geneva: World Health Organization.

Bowlby, J. (1953) *Child Care and the Growth of Love*. Harmondsworth: Penguin.

Bowlby, J. (1973) *Attachment and Loss, Vol. 2: Separation, Anxiety and Anger*. New York, NY: Basic Books.

Bowlby, J. (1981) *Attachment and Loss, Vol. 3: Sadness and Depression*. New York, NY: Basic Books.

Brazelton, T.B., Koslowski, B. and Main, M. (1974) "The origins of reciprocity: The early mother–infant interaction." In M. Lewis and L. Rosenblum (eds) *The Effect of the Infant on Its Caregiver*. New York, NY: Wiley, pp.49–77.

Brodzinsky, A.B. (1986) *The Mulberry Bird*. Indianapolis, IN: Perspectives Press.

Cain, B. and Patterson, A. (1990) *Double-Dip Feelings*. Washington D.C.: American Psychological Association.

Cassidy, J. and Berlin, L.J. (1994) "The insecure/ambivalent pattern of attachment: Theory and research." *Child Development 65*, 971–991.

Chrouso, G., Charmandari, E., Kino, R. and Souvatzoglou, E. (2003) "Pediatric stress: Hormonal regulators and human development." *Hormone Research 59*, 4, 161–179.

Cozolino, L. (2002) *The Neuroscience of Psychotherapy: Building and Rebuilding the Human Brain*. New York, NY: W.W. Norton.

de Bellis, M.D., Baum, A.S., Eccard, C.H., Boring, A.M., Jenkins, F.J. and Ryan, N.D. (1999a) "A.E. Bennett research award. Developmental traumatology. Part I: Biological stress systems." *Biological Psychiatry 45*, 10, 1259–1270.

de Bellis, M.D., Keshavan, M.S., Clark, D.B., Casey, B.J. et al. (1999b) "A.E. Bennett research award. Developmental traumatology. Part II: Brain development." *Biological Psychiatry 45*, 10, 1271–1284.

de Saint-Exupéry, A. (1943) *The Little Prince.* New York, NY: Harcourt.

Deaver, J.R. (1989) *Say Goodnight, Gracie.* New York, NY: Harper Trophy, First Keypoint Edition.

Dreikur, R. and Stolz, V. (1987) *Children: The Challenge.* New York, NY: Plume Books.

Ekman, P. (1999) "Facial expressions." In T. Dalgleish and T. Power (eds) *The Handbook of Cognition and Emotion* (pp.301–320). Chichester: John Wiley and Sons.

Ekman, P. (2001) *Telling Lies: Clues to Deceit in the Marketplace, Politics, and Marriage.* New York, NY: W.W. Norton.

Ekman, P. and Rosenberg, E. (2005) *What the Face Reveals: Basic and Applied Studies of Spontaneous Expression Using the Action Coding System (FACS).* New York, NY: Oxford University Press.

Erikson, E. (1963) *Childhood and Society* (2nd edition). New York, NY: W.W. Norton.

Fleming, S.J. and Adolph, R. (1986) "Helping bereaved adolescents: An empirical study." *Social Casework 60*, 547–551.

Freud, A. (1948) *The Ego and the Mechanics of Defence.* London: Hogarth Press.

Gogtay, N., Giedd, J.N., Lusk, L., Hayashi, K.M. *et al.* "Dynamic mapping of human cortical development during childhood through early adulthood." *Proceedings of the National Academy of Sciences 101*, 21, 8174–8179.

Goleman, D. (1995) *Emotional Intelligence.* New York, NY: Bantam.

Goleman, D. (2006) *Social Intelligence: The New Science of Human Relationships.* New York, NY: Bantam.

Gregory, V. (1992) *Through the Mickle Woods.* Boston, MA: Little, Brown and Co.

Grollman, S. (1988) *Shira: A Legacy of Courage.* New York, NY: Random House.

Gunnar, M.R. (2005) "Attachment and stress in early development: Does attachment add to the potency of social regulators of infant stress?" In C.S. Carter, L. Ahnert, K.E. Grossmann, S.B. Hrdy *et al.* (eds) *Attachment and Bonding: A New Synthesis.* Cambridge, MA: MIT Press, pp.245–255.

Harlow, H.F. and Harlow, M.K. (1966) "Social deprivation in monkeys." In M.L. Hainowitz and N.R. Hainowitz (eds) *Human Development.* New York, NY: Thomas Y. Crowell.

Hartmann, E. (1982) "Effects of L-tryptophan on sleepiness and on sleep." *Journal of Psychiatric Research 17*, 2, 107–113.

Havighurst, R.J. and DeHann, R.F. (1957) *Educating Gifted Children.* Chicago, IL: University of Chicago Press.

Hebb, D.O. (1949) *The Organization of Behavior: A Neuropsychological Theory.* New York, NY: Wiley.

Hofer, M.A. (1984) "Relationships as regulators: A psychobiological perspective on bereavement." *Psychosomatic Medicine 46*, 183–197.

Hofer, M.A. (1996) "On the nature and consequences of early loss." *Psychosomatic Medicine 58*, 570–581.

Houston, J. and Warnock, L. (1999) *Traumatic Brain Injury in Children and Teens: A National Guide for Families*. Wolfboro, NH: Lash and Associates.

Ingersoll, R.G. (1892) *The Ghosts and Other Lectures*. New York, NY: C.P. Farrell.

Kates, B.J. (1999) *We're Different, We're the Same*. Minneapolis, MN: Rebound by Sagebrush.

Kopp, M.S. and Rethelyi, J. (2004) "Where psychology meets physiology: Chronic stress and premature mortality—the Central-Eastern European health paradox." *Brain Research Bulletin 62*, 351–367.

Krystal, J.H., Bremner, J.D., Southwick, S.M. and Charney, D.S. (1998) "The emerging neurobiology of dissociation: Implication for treatment of posttraumatic stress disorder." In J.D. Bremner and C.R. Marmar (eds) *Trauma, Memory, and Dissociation* (pp.321–363). Washington D.C.: American Psychiatric Press.

Kübler-Ross, E. (1969) *On Death and Dying*. New York, NY: Macmillan.

LeDoux, J. (1996) *The Emotional Brain: The Mysterious Underpinnings of Emotional Life*. New York, NY: Simon and Schuster.

Luecken, L.J. (1998) "Childhood attachment and loss experiences affect adult cardiovascular and cortisol function." *Psychosomatic Medicine 60*, 765–772.

Luecken, L.J. (2000) "Parental caring and loss during childhood and adult cortisol responses to stress." *Psychology and Health 15*, 6, 841–851.

Luecken, L.J., Appelhans, B.M., Kraft, A. and Brown, A. (2006) "Never far from home: A cognitive-affective model of the impact of early-life family relationships on physiological stress responses in adulthood." *Journal of Social and Personal Relationships 23*, 2, 189–203.

Mahler, M.S., Pine, F., and Pergman, A. (1975) *The Psychological Birth of the Human Infant: Symbiosis and Individuation*. New York: Basic Books.

Maunder, R.G. and Hunter, J.J. (2001) "Attachment and psychosomatic medicine: Developmental contributions to stress and disease." *Psychosomatic Medicine 63*, 556–567.

Meany, M.J. (2001) "Maternal care, gene expression and the transmission of individual differences in stress reactivity across generations." *Annual Review of Neuroscience 24*, 1161–1192.

Miller, K.A. (2000) *Did My First Mother Love Me?* Portland, OR: Independent Publishing Group.

Moffat, M.J. (1992) *In the Midst of Winter: Selections from the Literature of Mourning*. New York: Vantage Press.

Moody, R.A. and Moody, C.P. (1991) "A family perspective: Helping children acknowledge and express grief following the death of a parent." *Death Studies 15*, 587–602.

Munsch, R.N. (1995) *Love You Forever*. Westport, CN: Firefly Books.

National Center for Infant Programs (1987–8) *Zero to Three: Bulletin of the National Center for Clinical Infant Programs VIII*, 1–5, (September 1987-June 1988) Washington: National Center for Infant Programs.

O'Conner, T.G. (2005) "Attachment disturbances associated with early severe deprivation." In C.S. Carter, L. Ahnert, K.E. Grossmann, S.B. Hrdy *et al.* (eds) *Attachment and Bonding: A New Synthesis*. Cambridge, MA: MIT Press, pp.257–267.

Panksepp, J. (1998) *Affective Neuroscience: The Foundations of Humans and Animal Emotions*. New York, NY: Oxford University Press.

Parkes, C.M. (1983) *Recovery from Bereavement*. New York, NY: Basic Books.

Paterson, K. (1977) *Bridge to Terabithia*. New York, NY: Harper Trophy.

Perry, B.D. (1993) "Neurodevelopment and the psychophysiolgy of trauma I: Conceptual consideration for clinical work with maltreated children." *APSAC Advisor* 6, 1, 1–18.

Perry, B.D. (1997) "Incubated in terror: Neurodevelopmental factors in the 'cycle of violence.'" In J. Osofsky (ed.) *Children in a Violent Society*. New York, NY: Guilford Press, pp.1240–1249.

Pesonen, A., Raikkonen, K., Heinonen, K., Kajantie, E., Forsen, T. and Eriksoon, J.G. (2007) "Depressive symptoms in adults separated from their parents as children: A natural experiment during World War II." *American Journal of Epidemiology 166*, 10, 1126–1133.

Pumpian-Mindlin, E. (1970) *Psychoanalysis as Science: The Hixon Lectures on the Scientific Status of Psychoanalysis*. Westport, CT: Greenwood Press.

Reich, W. (1945) *The Sexual Revolution: Toward a Self-Governing Character Structure* (3rd edition). New York, NY: Oregon Institute Press.

Riedler, B. (1999) *It's Time to Let You Know*. Silver City, NM: Global Relations Centers, Inc.

Scaer, R. (2005) *The Trauma Spectrum: Hidden Wounds and Human Resiliency*. New York, NY: W.W. Norton.

Schoettle, M. (2000) *W.I.S.E. Up Powerbook*. Burtonsville, MD: Center for Adoption Support and Education.

Schore, A.N. (1994) *Affect Regulation and the Origin of the Self: The Neurobiology of Emotional Development*. Mahwah, NJ: Lawrence Erlbaum Associates.

Schore, A.N. (2003a) *Affect Dysregulation and Disorders of the Self*. New York, NY: W.W. Norton.

Schore, A.N. (2003b) *Affect Regulation and the Repair of the Self*. New York, NY: W.W. Norton.

Shand, A.F. (1914) *The Foundations of Character*. London: Macmillan.

Shles, L. (1987) *Hugs and Shrugs: The Continuing Saga of a Tiny Owl Named Squib*. Rolling Hills Estates, CA: Jalmar Press.

Shura, M.F. (1988) *The Sunday Doll*. New York, NY: Dodd, Mead.

Siegel, D.J. (1999) *The Developing Mind*. New York, NY: Guilford Press.

Siegel, D.J. (2007) *The Mindful Brain: Reflection and Attunement in the Cultivation of Well-Being*. New York, NY: W.W. Norton.

Simon, N. (1993) *Why Am I Different?* Chicago, IL: Albert Whitman and Company.

Smedes, L.B. (1986) *How Can It Be All Right when Everything Is All Wrong?* New York, NY: Simon and Schuster.

Spitz, R.A. (1945a) "Analytic depression: An inquiry into the genesis of psychiatric conditions." In *Early Childhood, II*. New York, NY: International Universities Press.

Spitz, R.A. (1945b) "Hospitalism: An inquiry into the genesis of psychiatric conditions in early childhood." *The Psychoanalytic Study of the Child 1*, 1, 53–74.

Spitz, R.A. (1963) "Life and the dialogue." In R.N. Emde (ed) *René A. Spitz: Dialogues from Infancy—Selected Papers* (p.159). New York, NY: International Universities Press.

Stern, D.N. (1974) "Mother and infant at play: The dyadic interaction involving facial, vocal, and gaze behavior." In M. Lewis and L. Rosenblum (eds) *The Effect of the Infant on Its Caregiver*. New York, NY: Wiley, pp.187–213.

Stroebe, M. and Schut, H. (1999) "The dual process model of coping with bereavement: Rationale and description." *Death Studies 23*, 3, 197–224.

Sugar, M. (1968) "Normal adolescent mourning." *American Journal of Psychotherapy 22*, 2, 258–269.

Tolle, E. (2005) *A New Earth: Awakening to Your Life's Purpose*. New York, NY: Dutton.

van der Kolk, B.A., McFarline, A.C. and Weisaeth, L. (2006) *Traumatic Stress: The Effects of Overwhelming Experience in Mind, Body and Society*. New York, NY: Guilford Press.

van Gulden, H. and Bartels-Rabb, L.M. (1999) *Real Parents, Real Children: Parenting the Adopted Child*. New York, NY: Crossroad Publishing.

Waybill, A.M. (1974) *Chinese Eyes*. Telford, PA: Herald Press.

Weaver, I.C., Grant, R.J. and Meaney, M.J. (2002) "Maternal behavior regulates long-term hippocampal expression of BAX and apoptosis in the offspring." *Journal of Neurochemistry 82*, 998–1002.

Worden, J.W. and Silverman, P.R. (1996) "Parental death and the adjustment of school-age children." *Omega 33*, 91–102.

Ylvisaker, M. (1998) *Traumatic Brain Injury Rehabilitation: Children and Adolescents*. Boston, MA: Butterworth-Heinemann.

SUBJECT INDEX

AUTHOR INDEX